34116456

Joseph McCarthy

Joseph McCarthy

The Misuse of Political Power

By Daniel Cohen

THE MILLBROOK PRESS
BROOKFIELD, CONNECTICUT

Library of Congress Cataloging-in-Publication Data
Cohen, Daniel, 1936–
Joseph McCarthy : the misuse of political power / by Daniel Cohen.
p. cm.
Includes bibliographical references (p. 123) and index.
Summary: A biography of the Wisconsin senator whose questionable
methods as a "Communist witch-hunter" brought him fame in the decade
after World War II and led to his censure by the United States Senate.
ISBN 1-56294-917-9 (lib. bdg.)
1. Anti-Communist movements—United States—History—20th century—
Juvenile literature. 2. McCarthy, Joseph, 1908–1957—Juvenile
literature. 3. United States—Politics in government—1945–1953—
Juvenile literature. [1. McCarthy, Joseph, 1908–1957. 2. Legislators.
3. Anti-Communist movements—United States—History.
4. United States—Politics and government—1945–1953.] I. Title.
E743.5M2C65 1996 973.921'092—dc20 95-48314 CIP AC

Photographs courtesy of UPI/Corbis-Bettmann: pp. 8, 14, 20, 29, 35,
42, 57, 66, 70, 77, 83, 84, 89, 95, 96, 103, 107, 111; © 1954 Time Inc.
Reprinted by permission: p. 60; Herblock Cartoons © 1954 *The Washington
Post:* p. 100.

CONTENTS

Joseph
McCarthy

The 1954 Army-McCarthy hearings were a media event akin to the O.J. Simpson trial of the 90s. Citizens who had never watched a senate hearing before remained glued to their television sets day after day while the dramatic trial raged on for nearly three months.

INTRODUCTION

"Have You No Sense of Decency, Sir?"

In 1954 television was relatively new in the United States. Many people still didn't have TV sets. Yet between April 22 and June 17, millions of people watched what came to be called the Army-McCarthy hearings on TV. Those who didn't have sets often gathered in appliance stores where television sets were sold and displayed, in order to watch the drama unfold live. More people listened to the hearings on the radio. The hearings consumed a total of 187 hours of air time. There had never been anything like them in America before.[1]

The hearings, held in the elaborately decorated caucus room on the third floor of the Senate Office Building,[2] had been called to air a dispute between the U.S. Army and Joseph R. (everyone called him Joe) McCarthy, the junior senator from Wisconsin.

For several years Senator McCarthy had been charging that Communists held positions of power and influence in many American institutions, and particularly in the federal government. He had developed a large and enthusiastic following, not only in his home state but throughout the country. There were also many people who disagreed with him and considered him a dangerous fraud. But often they would not speak out against him because they were afraid that he would label *them* Communists. Even if there was not a shred of evidence to back up the charge, an attack like that from McCarthy could ruin a person's career. It had happened before.

McCarthy had attacked the Democratic party (he was a Republican), the State Department, and the Protestant churches, and then he began warning of Communist influence in the Army. That charge was so explosive that the U.S. Senate finally decided to hold public hearings on the matter.

The hearings had originally been scheduled to last about two weeks.[3] They dragged on for nearly three months. The American public had become fascinated by the spectacle. The dramatic high point of the hearings came on June 9. McCarthy's brash and aggressive young assistant, Roy Cohn, was being questioned by the Army's chief counsel, Boston attorney Joseph N. Welch. Welch had an easygoing, folksy, and deceptively gentle manner. In reality he was a tough and skilled questioner who could demolish a witness.

Cohn was in trouble. As he had done so often before, McCarthy tried to disrupt a line of questioning that was making his people look bad, by throwing out his own accusations. He launched into a tirade against Fred Fisher, a young member of Welch's law firm. McCarthy said Fisher was a member of a "Communist organization" and that Welch had tried to "foist him on the committee" where he could be "looking over secret and classified material."

When Fisher had been a law student, and for a few months afterward, he had been a member of the National Lawyers Guild, an organization that some believed was influenced by Communists. Fisher had long since quit the Guild and was, in fact, secretary of the Young Republicans' League. Welch had been looking for some assistants to come to Washington to help with the Army-McCarthy hearings. Fisher had been recommended, but when he told Welch about his past membership in the Lawyers Guild, Welch decided that it would not be a good idea for him to join the team in Washington. He told the young lawyer, "One of these days that will come out and go over national television and it will just hurt like the dickens." So Fisher went back to Boston.

McCarthy's charge was entirely fraudulent. Welch had never tried to "foist" Fisher on the committee. The entire story of Fisher's past and Welch's reaction had already appeared in the newspapers. What is more, just two days before the senator had launched his attack, both he and Cohn agreed not to go into the matter if Welch would agree not to bring up Cohn's military history (he had flunked the physical test for West Point). But McCarthy just couldn't stop himself.[4]

The attack was a huge mistake. McCarthy's supporters on the committee and in the hearing room knew it. Even Roy Cohn tried to stop him. But McCarthy plunged ahead, apparently enjoying himself. It was the sort of bully-boy role that he had played very successfully many times before. This time it was different.

When McCarthy finished, Welch struck back. "Until this moment, Senator," he began, "I think I never really gauged your cruelty or your recklessness."

The mild-looking Boston attorney then went on to explain about Fred Fisher. "I fear he shall always bear a scar needlessly inflicted by you. If it were in my power to forgive you for your reckless cruelty, I would do so. I like to think I am a gentleman, but your forgiveness will have to come from someone other than me."

McCarthy tried to resume his attack on Fisher, but Welch wouldn't let him get started.

"Let us not assassinate this lad further, Senator. You have done enough. Have you no sense of decency, sir, at long last? Have you left no sense of decency?"

There was a short, stunned silence, and then the room rocked with applause. Even the photographers, for the first time in the memory of Washington observers, dropped their cameras and clapped for Welch. Senator Karl Mundt (Republican from Nevada) who was chairing the hearing and had been a staunch supporter of McCarthy, determined to stop any anti-McCarthy outbursts but could do nothing. When the applause died down, he called a recess.[5]

McCarthy was stunned. He didn't seem to know what had hit him. As spectators and reporters left the room, they shunned the senator. They wouldn't speak to him. McCarthy looked around the room and said, "What did I do wrong?"

In a few brief years Joe McCarthy had risen from obscurity to become one of the most powerful and most feared men in America. The term "McCarthyism" became part of our political language. But after June 9, 1953, his decline was even faster than his rise.

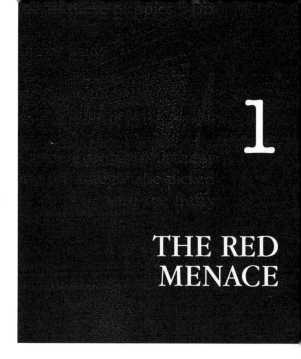

THE RED MENACE

Joe McCarthy was not one of those great leaders who, for good or ill, are able to shape events. He never founded a political party or even a political movement. And there is no indication that he ever really wanted to. He liked the attention and the power he achieved by his rhetoric, but there is some doubt that he even believed much of what he said. He was really more of a symbol of his time than a leader.

McCarthy rose to power in the United States on the strength of the claim that he was exposing Communist influence in the country and that he was protecting America from the "Red Menace." Red was the color associated with international communism.

While no one in America ever exploited the fear of communism more ruthlessly than McCarthy, he certainly didn't invent the technique, and he was not the only politician to use it.

Alleged "Reds and Bolsheviks," arrested in a November 1919 raid on New York City's Battery district, are shown leaving police wagons. They are on their way to Ellis Island where they will be held pending deportation proceedings.

Most Americans had despised and feared communism, particularly since the Russian Revolution in 1917, when the Communists took over the vast territory of Russia and transformed it into the Soviet Union. With the active support of the Soviet Union, communism became a powerful political and intellectual movement throughout much of the world. Even the United States had a small but active minority who were attracted to communism and its promise of a more equitable society. But communism was never really a major political force in the United States. Even at its height the American Communist party probably never had more than about 50,000 members. The actual influence of communism in America was greatly exaggerated both by the Communists themselves and by their enemies. People on the left or liberal side of the political spectrum might be labeled Communists or Communist sympathizers, even if they were anti-Communists.

In 1919, the same year a Communist party was organized in the United States, an ambitious U.S. attorney general, A. Mitchell Palmer, began a furious legal assault on those suspected of harboring radical left-wing ideas.[1] Communist party headquarters and those of other radical organizations were raided by the police and federal agents. Thousands of people were arrested. Some 249 aliens, individuals from other countries who were not U.S. citizens, were deported to Russia. A wide variety of anti-Communist state laws were passed; political meetings were broken up. There were beatings of suspected radicals, even an occasional lynching. The Bill of Rights of the Constitution, which gives people the right to hold unpopular political opinions, was ignored by some of the highest law-enforcement officials in the nation. The frenzy whipped up by what came to be called the "Palmer Raids" soon passed. But this brief and ugly episode was an indication of how deep the fear of the "Red Menace" was in a large segment of the American public and how easily it could be exploited.

In 1938 the U.S. House of Representatives created the Special Committee on Un-American Activities. The committee was later known simply as the House Un-American Activities Committee, or HUAC. The committee was first headed by the ultraconservative Texas Democrat Martin Dies and was often called the Dies Committee.[2] The committee made no real attempt to distinguish between Communists, Socialists, liberals, and other non-Communists who were on the political left. The committee charged that 1,121 government workers were "sympathetic with totalitarian ideology," and for its members that meant communism. Just how this figure was arrived at was never clear. The Dies Committee also condemned the administration of the liberal Democratic president Franklin Delano Roosevelt (FDR) for "coddling" Reds and being "soft" toward the Soviet Union. These charges were given wide publicity by conservative newspapers and commentators who had always hated the Roosevelt administration. A dozen years later Senator Joe McCarthy was to make almost identical charges against the administration of Roosevelt's successor, Harry S. Truman.

In 1941, when the United States entered World War II, public attitudes toward the Soviet Union and communism changed dramatically, if temporarily. The Soviet Union had become America's ally in the war against Hitler's Germany. But the forces of militant anti-communism did not disappear during the war.

Many of the laws that had been passed to curb the activities of pro-German groups during the war were broadened to include groups deemed to be pro-Communist as well.

When the war against Germany ended in 1945 the temporary allies, the United States and the Soviet Union, plunged almost immediately into that long period of mutual suspicion, hostility, and fear known as the Cold War. The Cold War ended only with the collapse of communism and the dissolution of the Soviet Union in 1990.

The popular FDR died shortly before World War II ended, and Vice President Harry S. Truman took over. But Truman was neither particularly well known nor well liked at the time. His opponents, both Republicans and conservative Southern Democrats, derided Truman as a hack politician (he had been a senator from Missouri before being picked as Roosevelt's vice president) and a bumbler who lacked the stature to be president. The old "soft on communism" charge was revived almost immediately. Though history has shown that Harry Truman was anything but "soft on Communism," the accusation was made frequently and it worried him a great deal.

In the 1946 midterm elections the Democrats in Congress were badly defeated. The defeat was blamed, at least in part, on the "soft on Communism" label that had been pinned on many Democratic candidates. Richard M. Nixon, a little-known Republican from California, won his first election to the U.S. House of Representatives in the 1946 election. The cornerstone of his successful campaign was his charge that his liberal Democratic opponent had Communist sympathies.

A worried Harry Truman then tried to outdo his critics in the field of anti-communism. He was going to show the American public that he was even harder on Communists than his critics. On March 21, 1947, the President set up a loyalty-oath security program within the government. A person didn't have to be a member of the Communist party to lose his or her government job. All that was necessary was "membership in, association with, or sympathetic affiliation with any organization, movement, group or combination of persons, designated by the Attorney General as . . . subversive." In practice, people could be fired from government jobs just because some anonymous informer said that they were subversive.

From the traditional position of the government having to prove guilt, the burden had shifted. The accused persons now had to prove their innocence, often without knowing the source of the charges. This loyalty and security program was a complete reversal of traditional American values. Some members of the Truman administration questioned the wisdom of such a program. President Truman himself may have had reservations about it. But once the order had been issued, the climate of fear and suspicion over who was a "subversive" increased measurably. The existence of the program itself seemed to lend credence to the idea that the federal government was riddled with subversives. There was no going back now.

One sure sign that the Truman loyalty program had inflamed rather than defused the "Red Menace" issue was a series of spectacular hearings on the Hollywood film industry by the House Un-American Activities Committee. The committee was now chaired by J. Parnell Thomas, and included Republican congressmen

Richard Nixon and Karl Mundt of South Dakota. They were both to play a role in the later career of Joe McCarthy.

One of the themes of the hearings was that "some of the most flagrant Communist propaganda films were produced as a result of White House pressure" during World War II. Many prominent Hollywood personalities appeared as "friendly" witnesses to denounce communism and sometimes to denounce their colleagues. Among the friendly witnesses was an actor who later turned politician and became president of the United States, Ronald Reagan.[3]

Witnesses who were not cooperative, who would not discuss their political views and associations, and who would not give the names of others they believed to be associated with subversive ideas or organizations were sometimes indicted. Ten of them, mostly screenwriters who were popularly called the "Hollywood Ten," actually went to jail as a result of their refusal to cooperate with HUAC. It is important to keep in mind that HUAC was not investigating spying or any other illegal activity. Its aim was to publicly expose people's political views and associations.

In the climate of fear and near hysteria that existed at that time, jail was not the only punishment for an individual suspected of being somehow associated with communism. Unlike the federal government, Hollywod had no official Loyalty Program. But there was the unofficial blacklist, which was just as effective in depriving people of their jobs. The executives of the major studios decreed that anyone who was even rumored to have subversive associations—and the term subversive was used very broadly—would no longer be given employment in the movie industry.[4]

Film celebrities (*from left to right*) Paul Henried, Lauren Bacall, Danny Kaye, and Humphrey Bogart are pictured here during a 1947 trip to Washington, D.C. for the purpose of protesting the House Un-American Activities Committee's method of probing alleged communism in Hollywood.

The careers of many actors, writers, directors, and others were either destroyed or severely curtailed. Some fled to Europe to continue their careers. Others went to Broadway, where there was no active blacklist. Some writers continued to produce movie scripts, but did so under assumed names. And a few, faced with the destruction of their careers, committed suicide. None of those who were blacklisted was actually accused of committing any crime, and most were not even members of the Communist party. They suffered because they held, or were believed to hold, political views that had become dangerously unpopular.

Nor was Hollywood the only place where a blacklist existed. There were blacklists in the radio and television industries, in many large and small corporations, in local governments, in universities, even in public school systems. Practically anywhere in America the label "Communist" or "subversive" could ruin a person.

Harry Truman scored a dramatic come-from-behind victory in the 1948 presidential election, defeating Republican challenger Thomas Dewey, governor of New York. But for all its drama the victory was a narrow one. Truman remained an unpopular president, and the cry that the government was filled with Communist agents was still raised and widely believed.

In 1949 a number of events occurred that made this charge seem even more credible. In January the pro-American Nationalist government of China, headed by Chiang Kai-shek, fled the mainland of China for the island now called Taiwan. There he established what he called the Republic of China. This left the mainland of China, the most populous nation on earth, under the control of the Communists headed by Mao Tse-tung.

For many years the Chinese Nationalists had been given a great deal of financial and other support by the United States. Yet their government had crumbled. It had been both out of touch with the Chinese people and corrupt. But Chiang and his Nationalists had a large number of very wealthy and influential supporters in the United States. These supporters were generally known as the China Lobby. The China Lobby insisted that it was not Chiang's fault that his government had been driven out of power. They said that the fault lay with the unwise and possibly traitorous actions of some U.S. government officials who had not given the Nationalists enough support. The cry went up that the U.S. government had somehow "lost" China. The fact that China had never been America's to win or lose was never really considered.[5]

Then on September 23, 1949, President Truman announced that the Soviets had exploded an "atomic device." That meant that they were on the threshold of developing the atomic bomb. What had once been called the "secret" of the atomic bomb was a secret no longer. This came as a tremendous shock to most Americans, who had been led to believe that the Russians were a bunch of ignorant peasants and that the Soviet government was incapable of matching the United States in science and technology. In fact, while the Soviet government was inefficient in many ways, it was effective in the development of military technology. But many Americans came to believe that the "secret" of the atomic bomb had been stolen by Communist spies. Information provided by spies certainly played some part in the development of the Soviet atomic weapons program, but their own highly trained scientists played a much larger part.

The fact that the Soviets, the number one enemy of the United States, now possessed atomic weapons, meant that not only could the United States destroy Russia, but Russia could also destroy the United States. World War II, which was fresh in everyone's memory, had been horrible. World War III, it seemed, would be far worse.

A few months later, on January 31, 1950, President Truman said that since the Soviets now had the atomic bomb it would be necessary for the United States to begin development of the so-called hydrogen or super bomb. Scientist Albert Einstein, whose work had laid the foundations for the nuclear age, warned that if such bombs were ever used they would lead to the "annihilation of any life on earth." The American people felt that they had just won a great war, that they had emerged from that war as the most powerful nation on earth—a nation whose supremacy should have been unchallenged. And now, just a few years later, Americans faced the prospect of a nuclear arms race and the possibility of a war in which even the winners would not survive.[6]

In schools all over the country students went through drills meant to teach them what they should do in case of nuclear attack. They were to dive under their desks and cover their heads with their clothes in order to protect themselves from the nuclear fallout. Very few believed that this "duck and cover" strategy would really work. People were scared. They were looking around for someone to blame.

Throughout 1949 the long, drawn-out trial of Alger Hiss, once an influential and respected member of both the Roosevelt and Truman administrations, had dragged on. Hiss had been accused of passing government secrets to the Soviets during the war. He was never tried for espionage, because there was not enough evidence for that charge. But since he had denied some of the accusations made against him under oath, he was brought to trial for lying under oath—the crime of perjury.

Hiss had his supporters, mostly among liberals and Democrats who had been his friends and co-workers. Those on the political right, mostly Republicans, were screaming for his blood. In the first Hiss trial the jury was unable to reach a verdict; it was a hung jury. But on January 21, 1950, just ten days before President Truman announced the need for the United States to develop a hydrogen bomb, a second jury convicted Alger Hiss. For many conservatives Alger Hiss became the living symbol of the treachery of the liberals and the Democrats. Hiss was sent to jail but continued to maintain his innocence. The Hiss case was one of the most divisive and controversial in American history. The facts of the case were still being argued with great passion almost half a century later.[7]

During the late 1940s the very air of Washington seemed polluted with intrigue and suspicion. And over it all hung the image of the mushroom cloud and total destruction from nuclear war with a powerful and implacable foe, "Godless communism." It was a fearful time. And this was the atmosphere in which Joe McCarthy thrived, briefly but spectacularly.

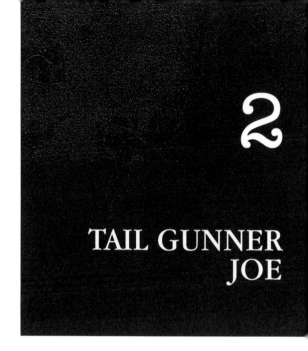

TAIL GUNNER JOE

Joseph Raymond McCarthy was born on November 14, 1908, in rural northern Wisconsin near the town of Appleton. The place, which was hardly even a town, was called Grand Chute. Joe was the fifth of seven children of Tim and Bridget McCarthy, a hardworking, second-generation Irish-American farm family. They lived in a simple white clapboard house with no electricity and no indoor plumbing. Simple as it was, the house was an improvement over the log cabin that the McCarthy family had lived in until shortly before Joe's birth.

Life was hard. Tim McCarthy worked fifteen hours a day, seven days a week, running his spread. And he expected his boys to do the same. He was a serious, no-nonsense farmer. By the time Joe McCarthy became famous, a lot of legends had grown up about his boyhood. According to some, he was a shy and introverted boy, gawky and unattractive, constantly bullied by his older brothers and ignored by his surly father. However, say the stories, he was his mother's favorite. She regarded him as the brightest of her children. She protected him, and that was a source of friction between his father and mother. Tim thought him quite ordinary, and believed that the boy was being coddled and spoiled by his doting mother.

But others insisted that, on the contrary, Joe McCarthy had been an extroverted and vigorous boy, very popular and regarded as handsome. The stories of family friction, they say, are not true. In this version of McCarthy's boyhood, his family was very close, and they always looked out for one another. Far from being bullied, Joe was physically tough and always ready for a fight.[1]

One thing everyone agreed on is that Joe McCarthy had a lot of energy. He worked very hard, even in a community known for its hard work. When he wasn't working on the farm, he was constantly on the go, running from place to place. He gulped his food and didn't sleep very much. He didn't seem able to sit still. Today he might be called "hyperactive."

All of this activity appears to have left young McCarthy prone to a variety of puzzling ailments, some real, some perhaps imaginary. This was a pattern of illness that was to plague him for the rest of his life.

Joe attended the local school, a cramped one-room structure that contained all eight grades under a single teacher. It was fairly typical of poor rural schools of the time. Joe was, by all accounts, a good but undisciplined student, with a remarkable memory. His greatest problem was an inability to keep his mouth shut. He was always blurting out answers, or asking questions at the wrong time.

Like his brothers, indeed like most of his school-mates, Joe quit school when he was fourteen. A high school education was rare in Grand Chute. This may have disappointed his mother, who thought Joe had the ability to "get ahead." But his father, who could always use another hand on the farm, regarded the decision as natural and probably inevitable. Why did a farmer need a high school diploma?[2]

Joe took up farming with his characteristic energy. But he also began to display his characteristic restlessness. In truth, farming bored him. He stuck it out for a couple of years and then decided that it was time to try some other line of work.

At the age of sixteen Joe took up raising chickens. At first, by sheer hard work and energy, the business appeared to succeed. But raising chickens is a risky business. At one point he became seriously ill with influenza, and by the time he recovered, his business had nearly been destroyed. He tried to rebuild, but his heart wasn't in it anymore.

Then he heard that a grocery chain was opening a new store in the small community of Manawa, just northwest of Appleton, and they were looking for a manager. Joe applied for the job and got it. At the age of twenty Joe McCarthy became a small-town grocer. And because he was ready to work harder and longer hours than anyone else, he was successful.

In Manawa, Joe took a room in the house of Mrs. Frank Osterloth, just across from the high school. Mrs. Osterloth persuaded Joe to go back to school and get a diploma. Joe certainly stood out among his high school classmates. He was twenty years old, nearly 6 feet tall (1.8 meters) and weighed 170 pounds (77 kilograms). But he had a quick mind, a retentive memory, and all that energy. He spent so much time on his schoolwork that he lost his supermarket job. But he barely seemed to notice. He supported himself by ushering at night in the local movie theater. He was able to finish four years of high school in a single year. According to the school principal, he worked so hard that "he nearly killed himself."

The restless young man had gone about as far as he could go in Manawa. It was time to move on. He enrolled in Marquette University, a well-known Jesuit college in Milwaukee. He began as an engineering student, but didn't like it and soon switched to law. In law he could use his good memory and quick tongue to the best advantage. He paid his bills by working at a variety of jobs: short-order cook, dish washer, whatever he could get. It was the Depression; jobs were hard to come by and the pay was low.

He also made money gambling. Joe played poker the way he did everything else—no holds barred. He raised the stakes so high and so fearlessly that opponents usually folded, even when they had better cards. A friend from his college days commented, "One should play poker with him to really know him." [3] .

Joe also boxed at Marquette. Boxing was popular at the school, and Joe was a crowd pleaser. He was nicknamed "Smiling Joe." He was known more for his ability to take a tremendous amount of punishment and keep on slugging than he was for his skill as a boxer. [4]

As a student he earned average grades. All in all, there was nothing remarkable about Joe's college career. Those who knew him at the time generally remembered him fondly. Outwardly he could be brash and aggressive. Some suspected that he was trying to make up for feelings of inferiority about his very humble back-

McCarthy is shown here as a student at Marquette University where his ability to cram was famous. With his part-time jobs and other outside activities, he didn't have time to keep up with his work. But as final exams loomed he was able to review an entire semester's work in a few intense days and nights of study and earn moderately good grades.

ground. To his close friends, the small circle that he trusted, he could be warm and friendly. Everyone who knew him commented on his desire to be liked and accepted.[5]

It was during college that Joe McCarthy first began to talk of his political ambitions. He didn't seem to hold any strong political ideas, but he believed that politics might be a good career. His desire to go into politics was to grow into an almost overpowering obsession.[6]

After getting his law degree in 1935, McCarthy set up his practice in the small town of Waupaca, Wisconsin, north of Appleton. He soon got the reputation of being a "hustler," the sort of lawyer who would chase after clients and take cases, like some divorce cases, that other lawyers in that conservative community might avoid. But the Depression was in full swing, and cases were hard to come by. McCarthy was chronically short of money, and not careful at handling what money he did have. And he was still a gambler. He would still play high-stakes poker, which he couldn't really afford. But the general impression was that McCarthy made more money gambling than he lost.

McCarthy certainly had his eye on politics. The way to get into politics in a small community was to join organizations and meet people. McCarthy joined everything from the softball team to the Chamber of Commerce, and he was active in every organization he joined.

Waupaca was a solid Republican town. Yet McCarthy chose to register as a Democrat. In a highly conservative area he became known as an outspoken supporter of the liberal president Franklin D. Roosevelt. Later, people assumed that he had done this not because of any strong political convictions, but because it was a lot easier to make a mark as a Democrat than as a Republican where you had much competition.

His Democratic party affiliation paid off quickly. He got a job in the office of Mike Eberlein, a prominent attorney from nearby Shawano. Eberlein was a conservative Republican. In small towns, lawyers of one party often try to get lawyers of the other party in their office for balance.

McCarthy soon became the most prominent Democrat in Shawano. In fact, he was practically the only Democrat in Shawano. He campaigned hard for Roosevelt in the 1936 election. He denounced the Republicans in terms that, some fifteen years later, McCarthy as a senator might regard as dangerously subversive. He also ran for district attorney on the Democratic ticket—his first try at elective office. He didn't stand a chance of winning, and he knew it. But the campaign gave him experience, and it got his name known around the area.

Two years later there was a more serious election, this time for circuit judge. It was a nonpartisan election, so McCarthy didn't have to run as a Democrat—which would have doomed his candidacy from the start. But there was a problem. His partner and friend Mike Eberlein also wanted the job. McCarthy simply announced his candidacy first. Eberlein was shut out. Later the two men made up and became friends again, but there was a lot of resentment at the time.[7]

McCarthy's opponent in the election was Edgar Werner, who had been a circuit court judge ever since the days of President Woodrow Wilson in World War I. Werner had a reputation for honesty and independence. When he decided to stand for reelection, everyone assumed that he would be an easy winner. Everyone, that is, except Joe McCarthy. Even McCarthy's friends thought he was crazy to try to unseat Werner. But it was in this 1939 campaign that Joe McCarthy first really displayed the political instincts and style that were to make him famous.

First, McCarthy attacked Judge Werner's age, saying that he was not really seventy-three but seventy-six years old. If challenged, McCarthy could admit that Werner was only seventy-three. In fact, Werner was actually sixty-six years old, and McCarthy knew it. McCarthy also attacked Werner for having a total worth of between $170,000 and $200,000—a huge sum in those days and in that place. But Werner made that money over a career of more than thirty years. His annual salary was average for an attorney at that time.

In using such tactics McCarthy didn't do anything that other politicians haven't done in running for office. He was just a bit bolder than most.

But what put McCarthy over was his energy. He was all over the district during the campaign, and probably shook the hand of every eligible voter at least once. He had an astonishing memory. He knew every farmer's name, his wife's name, his children's names, even the name of the family dog. He was a folksy campaigner—always urging people to "Call me Joe." He could talk about the crops and about the weather, and if need be he could milk a cow. Werner, on the other hand, hated campaigning. Many of the people in the district either had not seen him in years or had never seen him. Werner was a distant, austere man, the opposite of plain old "Joe." In the end McCarthy, who had been given no chance to win, swamped his opponent. Werner didn't know what hit him. After the election he retired from the practice of law and died a short time later.

At the age of twenty-nine Joe McCarthy was the youngest circuit judge that anyone could remember. He immediately began to establish a reputation for himself, not so much for his judicial skills but for his energy and speed. He worked practically around the clock, and cleared the backlog of cases before the court in a mere two months. He also got a reputation for granting "quickie" divorces. At that time getting a divorce often involved a long and difficult legal proceeding. According to one story he began hearing a divorce case while bounding up the courthouse steps with the attorneys alongside him. Within a few minutes the case was over.

The woman who was seeking the divorce was surprised at the speed. "But is that all there is to it?" she said. "I thought there would be a court trial."

"We're efficient around here," replied Judge McCarthy. "You wanted a divorce and now you have one."[8]

Later McCarthy was to become so controversial that it was difficult to determine just how much truth there was in these stories of his early career. Though he was free-wheeling and unorthodox, McCarthy seems to have been a popular judge. He wasn't pompous as so many judges were. He was a hard worker, and he got the job done quickly, bypassing legal red tape. People liked that.

McCarthy had no desire for a career in the law. In fact, being a judge bored him. What interested him was politics. He often told his friends that one day he would run for "real" political office. Judicial office wasn't "real" politics to McCarthy. By now McCarthy had become a Republican. There was not much political future for a Democrat in that part of Wisconsin. McCarthy spent a good deal of his free time traveling around the state getting to know and becoming known by important political figures. He even said that he didn't get married because marriage would interfere with his political career.

McCarthy's plans, and those of just about everyone else in the United States, were interrupted on December 7, 1941, when the Japanese bombed the U.S. naval base at Pearl Harbor in Hawaii. That act triggered America's entry into World War II. Early in June 1942, Joe McCarthy walked into a Marine recruiting office in Milwaukee and signed up. As a sitting judge McCarthy could have been exempted from military service. Perhaps, like many others, he volunteered strictly out of a feeling of patriotism. However, there is reason to believe that he also had politics on his mind. He knew the political value of a war record in a campaign.

McCarthy, who portrayed himself as an "ordinary guy," claimed that he had enlisted as a "buck private." In fact, he requested and received an officer's commission. For almost three years he served as an intelligence officer in the Pacific. His main job was to question pilots who returned from bombing runs over Japanese-held islands, to see if they had picked up any information that might be useful on future missions. It was a necessary job, and McCarthy performed credibly. But it was not the dangerous front-line action that he later claimed. He said that he flew many combat missions as a tail gunner. In truth, his only flights were on routine training missions, where there was almost no chance of

McCarthy at a plane's machine guns during the war.
There was nothing dishonorable about McCarthy's
wartime record as an interrogator of pilots returning
from bombing runs, but there was nothing special
about it either. Yet "Tail Gunner Joe" managed to
build a reputation as a war hero.

enemy action. Everyone flew the routine missions when they could, just to relieve the boredom.

He was quick to send information about his service to the papers back home. The information wasn't always accurate. One claim that was publicized in the newspapers back in Wisconsin was that McCarthy had broken the record for the most ammunition used in a single mission. That was true—sort of. What the papers did not write, and did not know, was that he was shooting at coconut trees because there were no enemy planes. McCarthy was just using up ammunition. His buddies even gave him a mock award for shooting up the island's plant life.

In his later political campaigns McCarthy would sometimes walk with a limp. He said that it was the result of a wartime injury. He once said that he carried "ten pounds of shrapnel" in his leg, a physical impossibility. He had been injured during the war. He broke his foot during some horseplay while aboard the ship *Chandeleur.*

Joe McCarthy wasn't the first politician to exaggerate his wartime exploits. And he wasn't the last. As in so many things, he was just a little bit more extreme than most. When he started running for higher office, he spoke of having participated in fourteen bombing missions. The figure rose regularly until it reached a high of thirty-two. He asked for and received a variety of medals, most of which he did not deserve. His early campaign posters pictured him in full flying gear, with an aviator's cap, and several belts of ammunition wrapped around him. He took pains to cultivate his "war hero" image with veterans groups, who later were to be among his strongest backers. In the end McCarthy may actually have come to believe some of his own "war hero" stories, for he had told them so many times. He certainly got many people to believe them.

While serving in the Pacific, McCarthy had a chance meeting with a young Navy lieutenant named John F. Kennedy. They never became friends, but the Kennedy family was to play a significant role in McCarthy's future political career.[9]

In the spring of 1944, Joe McCarthy, while still serving in the Pacific, decided to enter the Republican primary for the senatorial nomination. That puzzled a lot of Wisconsin Republicans, who weren't sure that he even was a Republican. If they remembered him at all, it was as a Roosevelt Democrat.

There were, however, more serious problems in his candidacy. McCarthy was still a sitting judge, and it was against the law in Wisconsin for a sitting judge to run for any office except a judicial one. The attorney general of Wisconsin decided that the problems could be sorted out after the election, if McCarthy won. (Since McCarthy did not win the election, the problem was never addressed.)

When McCarthy became an official candidate, he was a political novice who was in the Pacific some 9,000 miles (14,500 kilometers) from Wisconsin. His opponent was Alexander Wiley, a powerful incumbent senator and a canny politician. McCarthy was the longest of long shots. He obtained a thirty-day leave from the Marines in order to campaign. In Wisconsin he received something of a hero's welcome. The Shawano *Evening Leader* described his walk down Main Street: "[H]e did not have to walk far to find a friend. It was 'Hello, Joe' left and right, to the young judge who left a seat on the bench . . . to take another . . . behind the rear guns of a dive bomber."[10]

McCarthy also appears to have violated some of Wisconsin's campaign financing laws. He funneled some of his own money through his relatives in an attempt to evade limits on the amount of money a candidate could contribute to his own campaign. In order to hide this, he did not file income tax returns in Wisconsin for 1943. But, once again, since he didn't win the election none of this legal corner cutting was ever pursued.

McCarthy didn't come near beating Wiley in the primary. But he did collect a respectable 80,000 votes, and came in second in a large field. He carried the three counties within his judicial district where he was well known. Joe McCarthy now had a solid political base. He could no longer be regarded as a hopeless long shot and unknown in Wisconsin politics.

McCarthy returned to the Pacific and immediately applied for another leave, claiming that he had to fulfill his judicial duties. When the leave was denied, he resigned his commission and applied for a discharge. This was granted in February 1945. Though the war was still far from over, the self-styled "war hero" had other things on his mind. Another Wisconsin senatorial seat was up for election in 1946. Within a month of his discharge, McCarthy began gearing up for the race that was to propel him onto the national scene.

3

THE JUNIOR SENATOR

In his next political race Joe McCarthy was to face a Wisconsin legend. His opponent in the Republican senatorial primary was Robert "Young Bob" La Follette. His father, Robert Marion "Fighting Bob" La Follette, had served three terms as governor and then was elected to the U.S. Senate in 1906, where he served for nineteen years until his death. He is still regarded as one of the most outstanding U.S. senators in history. In 1925, Young Bob easily won his father's vacant seat and became one of the youngest U.S. senators ever.

McCarthy campaigned mainly on his war record, real and imaginary. His slogan was "Congress Needs a Tail Gunner."[1] He complained that La Follette had not enlisted—failing to note that Bob La Follette was forty-six and too old for active duty in the military at the time that Pearl Harbor was bombed. La Follette had stayed behind in Washington throughout the war. But so had practically every other senator and congressman. As for his own political program, McCarthy was vague.

La Follette was not only legendary but powerful. Though running on the Republican ticket, he was a liberal and had close ties to the Roosevelt administration. This allowed him to distribute a lot of federal political patronage throughout Wisconsin. He was a senator who could "bring home the bacon" for his constituents and supporters.

Unlike his father, however, "Young Bob" La Follette did not have the common touch. He hated campaigning, and he liked Washington. He rarely returned to his native state. La Follette was consumed with national and international issues, which often seemed remote from the concerns of farmers, small businessmen, and laborers of Wisconsin. Though he had represented them for years, and his family name was familiar, the people of Wisconsin barely knew him. And the large conservative wing of the Republican party couldn't stand him. The conservatives had been plotting his downfall for years.[2]

Within Republican ranks, however, even the anti-La Follette forces were not sure that McCarthy was their strongest candidate. But he managed to outbluff or scare off potential rivals. The primary was to be strictly a La Follette–McCarthy battle. But as in his previous campaigns, even McCarthy's friends regarded him as a hopeless long shot. Yet McCarthy had accurately sensed La Follette's vulnerability, and, as before, his political instincts were shrewd and on target.

La Follette was convinced that he had the nomination wrapped up. All his friends and political advisers told him that this obscure judge didn't have a chance.

As a result La Follette had virtually no campaign organization in Wisconsin. He spent no money on the campaign and only returned to the state some ten days before the election. He was in Washington working on the Congressional Reorganization Act, a piece of legislation that he had been interested in for many years.

By contrast, Joe McCarthy was a whirlwind of activity in Wisconsin. No town was too small for him to visit, no distance too great for him to travel. He wore out the reporters who tried to cover his campaign. And no voters or potential voters were safe from McCarthy's handshake once he spotted them. He would grab them by the hand and say, "I don't want to lose your vote, sir. My name is McCarthy, I'm running for the Senate."

When the votes were tabulated, McCarthy had 207,935 and La Follette 202,557. If La Follette had taken McCarthy's challenge seriously and campaigned actively, he probably would have won. But like so many others, he had underestimated the hard-driving and ruthless McCarthy.[3]

McCarthy always regarded his victory in the Wisconsin Republican primary as one of his greatest political triumphs. And he was right. His victory against the Democratic candidate, Howard McMurray, was almost a foregone conclusion. McMurray was an uninspired campaigner. Wisconsin was a Republican state, and 1946 was a big Republican year.

On domestic issues McCarthy railed against government bureaucrats and government regulations. He was really campaigning against Roosevelt's New Deal, which he had so enthusiastically supported early in his political career. His positions were standard conservative Republican. On the subject of anti-communism,

His defeat by McCarthy was a political and personal
disaster for Robert "Young Bob" La Follette, shown
here in 1948. He never ran for office again. He
stayed around Washington doing a variety of political
tasks. His health declined, he became depressed, and
in 1953 he shot himself.

McCarthy hit hard against what he said was the "disloyalty" of the Democrats. "All Democrats are not Communists," he told one crowd. "But enough are voting the Communist way to make their presence in Congress a serious threat to . . . our nation." The charge, of course, was extreme. But it was also fairly standard Republican campaign rhetoric in 1946.

The Republican candidates swept the 1946 congressional elections, taking fifty-four House and eleven Senate seats. One of those new Republican senators was Joseph R. McCarthy, who became the junior senator from Wisconsin.

When McCarthy first arrived in Washington, he didn't make much of an impression. With a freshman class of better-known fire-breathing anti-Communist conservative legislators like Richard Nixon, John Bricker (Republican from Ohio), and William Jenner (Republican from Indiana), Joe McCarthy might almost have been mistaken for a moderate. The truth was that nobody knew McCarthy's real views, or if he had any strongly held convictions at all, beyond the obvious desire to be elected to office.[4]

The press took some note of his relative youth—he was thirty-eight, ten years younger than the average senator—and of his hard-driving style. When he spoke on the Senate floor he often played fast and loose with the facts. Since he wasn't an important senator, no one cared much.

McCarthy did not fit easily into the Washington social life. He was still a small-town farm boy. A "country bumpkin," said one reporter who knew him. He either didn't know or didn't care about refinement and good manners. He could be crude and boastful.[5]

Even when McCarthy began to buy better clothes, his suits always looked rumpled and unpressed. He had a heavy beard, and no matter how often he shaved, he usually looked as if he needed a shave. That was a feature that McCarthy opponents were to caricature mercilessly in the future. He never settled into Washington. He lived in a series of rented rooms. "Just a place to hang my hat," he would say.

Rather than trying to fit in, McCarthy went out of his way to emphasize his differences with the Washington establishment. He played the tough Marine, the no-nonsense blue-collar guy, the self-made man. That was in stark contrast to many Washington insiders who came from well-to-do families, had gone to private schools and the best colleges, and belonged to country clubs. Some observers conjectured that Joe McCarthy believed that he was excluded from many Washington circles because of his humble background and that his best defense was to emphasize his blue-collar, masculine virtues. Others thought that McCarthy was playing a shrewd political game identifying himself with the "ordinary folks" against the Washington establishment, which most people did not trust anyway.

On a personal level he got on well with the people who worked in the Senate office building. He was friendly, accessible, and it was always "Call me Joe." There were loads of stories about his personal kindness and consideration.

In 1948, after the Senate recessed, McCarthy headed out to North Dakota, where he worked as a field hand during the wheat harvest. He took the job under an assumed name, so that no one would know who he was. He was popular with the other workers. When the owner of the farm finally did discover that his hired hand was a U.S. senator, he said, "It was a fine thing for him to do. I wish more of those high officials in Washington would do something like that and see our problems . . . at first hand." Was this a political gimmick? Probably. McCarthy surely was aware that his identity would become known and that the story would enhance his common-man image. But he also seems to have enjoyed the experience, and was more comfortable with the field hands than with many of his colleagues in Washington.[6]

One ominous development was McCarthy's drinking. Back in Wisconsin he had never been more than a moderate drinker. Once in Washington he began to consume alcohol in increasingly large quantities. Some people believed that this was the result of the increased pressures of his new life, or because of his separation from family and friends, and a sense of isolation in Washington. Whatever the reason, McCarthy frequently got drunk and obnoxious at Washington social functions. Many Washington hostesses didn't invite him to parties because they were afraid that he might cause a scene. There were many stories about his antics.

In his political life McCarthy was behaving like a man without a purpose. He certainly supported the agenda of the conservative Republicans. He denounced communism, Communists in the government, and the "Red Menace" quite regularly, but unlike congressmen such as Richard Nixon, anti-communism was not an issue with which McCarthy was particularly identified at this stage of his career.

One issue that McCarthy did become identified with was sugar prices. The issue was a complicated one, involving the lifting of wartime price controls on sugar and the size of the world sugar crop. Though Wisconsin did have a sugar-beet industry that was eager to have price controls lifted, this was not the sort of issue that was a natural for McCarthy, who disliked complicated and detailed problems. There were not enough sugar-beet growers in Wisconsin to influence him. But the soft-drink industry, which used a lot of sugar, was also interested in the issue. They had a more powerful lobby. McCarthy, who needed money, had obtained a $20,000 loan from a representative of the Pepsi-Cola Company. There was nothing illegal about this, but it looked suspicious and was the sort of issue that could create problems in a reelection campaign. Around Washington, McCarthy was often called the "Pepsi-Cola Kid."[7]

During a debate in the Senate on the issue of sugar price controls, McCarthy was caught in a flat-out lie, which was exposed by a fellow Republican. Undaunted, McCarthy tried to cover his tracks by telling another lie. He also behaved rudely and in a way that violated the unwritten rules of the Senate. Though he had been in Washington only for a few months, some of his colleagues were marking him down as unreliable and a potential troublemaker.[8]

McCarthy also developed a close relationship with the real estate lobby. He became a ferocious opponent of public housing, which was also opposed by the real estate interests. Later it was discovered that he had received $10,000 from a manufacturer of prefabricated homes who also opposed public housing. The money allegedly was for the right to distribute a pamphlet on housing that McCarthy was supposed to have written. In reality the pamphlet had been written by employees of the manufacturer. Payments of this sort were not, strictly speaking, illegal or against congressional rules at that time. Many other congressmen accepted money under similar circumstances. But such payments were rightly regarded with suspicion by the voters. Again, this was the sort of issue that could be embarrassing in a political campaign.

The most bizarre episode in McCarthy's early senatorial career came in the investigation of what was called the "Malmédy massacre." In the closing days of World War II the German army overwhelmed several hundred American soldiers near the Belgian village of Malmédy. More than seventy of the disarmed survivors were machine-gunned to death. After the war seventy-three of Hitler's elite SS troops were found guilty by an American war-crimes trial, and forty-three of them were sentenced to be hanged for the massacre. There was a long series of legal delays. The condemned men claimed that confessions had been beaten out of them by sadistic American prosecutors.

The whole affair was eventually the subject of a hearing by a subcommittee of the Senate Armed Services Committee. While McCarthy was not a member of the committee, he threw himself right into the hearing and on the side of the S.S. defendants and against the U.S. Army. He badgered witnesses, yelled at other senators, made a series of unsupportable and often demonstrably false statements, and finally and dramatically walked out claiming that the committee was trying to "whitewash" the Army.

It was incredible, just the sort of McCarthy performance that all Americans were to become familiar with in the years to come. But why did he do it at this time, and in this case? Defending S.S. men accused of murdering American soldiers was not a way to win popularity in 1949. His diatribes against other senators so irritated his colleagues that the members of the Armed Services Committee took the unusual step of passing a resolution condemning the attacks he made on the chairman of the subcommittee as "utterly undeserved."

The subcommittee did exonerate the Army. In a report, it concluded that while there were some minor judicial abuses, on the whole the Germans had been treated fairly. Ultimately the death sentences of the surviving Germans were commuted to life imprisonment, and by the late 1950s they had all been released.

Historians have puzzled over why a shrewd politician like Joe McCarthy chose to conduct such a vigorous and public defense of Nazi soldiers. No matter what his enemies thought of him, there is no evidence that he secretly harbored Nazi sympathies. There was nothing in his history to indicate any concern for the rights of the accused, no matter how despised and unpopular they might be. The best guess is that McCarthy was pushed into the Malmédy hearings by some wealthy German-American families in Wisconsin who did have Nazi sympathies or at least felt that the hearings would inflame anti-German sentiment in America. McCarthy threw himself into the task with his characteristic zeal, and overdid it.[9]

His behavior toward other senators caused even conservative Republicans who should have been his natural allies to shun him. Back home the Malmédy affair, the Pepsi-Cola Kid label, and the old stories about his running a "divorce mill" when he was judge, which had now resurfaced, began to take their toll. His popularity was sinking fast. Though he wasn't up for reelection until 1952, he was already being marked down as a "loser." Other Republicans were beginning to plan a primary challenge.

So it was that at the beginning of 1950, Joe McCarthy's young political career was already in serious trouble. He needed something to revive his fortunes. He needed an issue. One enduring Washington legend is that McCarthy found his issue on January 7, 1950, at a dinner with three conservative friends. According to the story, McCarthy discussed his political problems and said that he was searching for a reelection issue with "sex appeal." A number of issues were discussed, and finally one of the men suggested, "communism in government." McCarthy jumped at it. "The government is full of Communists," he is supposed to have said. "The thing to do is to hammer at them."

The dinner on January 7 did take place. But if "communism in government" was discussed, and if so to what extent, has been a matter of dispute. In fact, the issue of "communism in government" was not new to McCarthy. He had used it in his senatorial campaign. He had made speeches on the subject prior to January 7, 1950. Many other Republicans, Richard Nixon most notably, had already used the issue far more successfully than McCarthy had.[10]

Nor did he immediately adopt the issue. Over the next few weeks McCarthy had little to say about the "Red Menace." It is more likely that he had no plan to make this the hallmark of his career. He just fell into it. And fall he did.

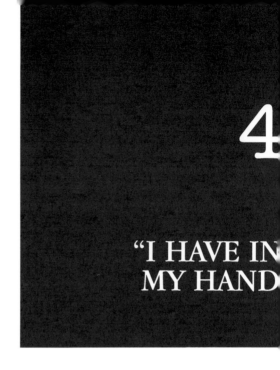

4

"I HAVE IN
MY HAND

In February 1950, Senator Joe McCarthy was scheduled to deliver a series of Lincoln Day speeches at Republican meetings throughout the country. Speeches of this sort were considered a party obligation. McCarthy appeared to attach no particular significance to this speech-making trip. As a junior senator, and one who was very much out of favor with the Republican congressional powers, he was not given any major speaking assignments. He was sent to speak to small groups in small cities.

On February 9 he was to address a county Women's Republican Club in Wheeling, West Virginia. The speech was fairly standard anti-Communist fare. Some of it was taken almost directly from a recent speech by Richard Nixon. It blamed the "traitorous actions" of many in the government. But McCarthy added his own touch.

"While I cannot take the time to name all of the men in the State Department who have been named as members of the Communist Party and members of a spy ring, I have here in my hand a list of 205 . . . a list of names that were known to the Secretary of State . . . and who nevertheless are still working and shaping the policy of the State Department."[1]

It was a pure McCarthy bluff. He had no list. The figure of 205 had been given more than three years earlier by the secretary of state, and referred to the number of State Department employees about whom "damaging information" had been uncovered during a loyalty screening. There was no indication of what sort of "damaging information" had been found. It could have been about their drinking or about their sex lives. And there was no indication of how many of them still worked for the State Department. They certainly were not all policymakers. McCarthy made it sound as if he was actually holding a list of 205 Soviet spies with top jobs in the State Department.

The speech was fairly well received by the partisan audience, but did not appear to attract an unusual amount of attention. But the next night he gave essentially the same speech in Salt Lake City, Utah. This time the figures had changed. Now he said he had the names of "57 card-carrying members of the Communist Party" who held high State Department positions and were "the shapers of American foreign policy." He didn't have 57 names either. The number 57 appears to have come from a document that was several years old. It contained the names of people about whom "derogatory information" had been received. The information covered a wide range. For example, in one case the subject was accused of "entertaining both Negroes and whites in her apartment." In 1950, Washington was still a largely segregated city, and such behavior would have been considered unusual. But it had nothing to do with spying. In another case the charge against the subject was that he was a heavy drinker. Many of the 57 on the list no longer even worked for the State Department. None of them were high enough to properly be called "shapers of American foreign policy."

But when McCarthy made the charges they sounded so serious and so specific that the press and his audiences began to take notice. When he repeated essentially the same speech at Reno, Nevada, there were gasps and a few tears of frustration and rage in the audience. Reporters began asking McCarthy for his list. He had a variety of excuses for not producing it. At one point he said that he had left it in his other suitcase. But reporters also began asking members of the Truman administration about the charges. The administration didn't know how to respond, because they didn't know what kind of information McCarthy had. Spokesmen waffled, and looked as if they were hiding something.

Suddenly Joe McCarthy was getting more attention than he had ever had. As far as he was concerned, he was onto a good thing and he was going to run with it.[2] On the afternoon of February 20, McCarthy took his charges to the floor of the U.S. Senate. There he delivered an almost eight-hour harangue. This time he was talking about "81 loyalty risks." Again, McCarthy's information came from old documents, and he twisted and exaggerated the information to suit his purposes. He was also dealing only with charges made by unnamed informants. Nothing had been proved against anyone.

The Democrats tried to knock holes in McCarthy's presentation, but they were poorly prepared for the attack. McCarthy kept throwing more names and charges at them until they were groggy. A few Republicans also objected to the performance. But most sat silent. Senator Robert Taft of Ohio, the conservative leader of the senatorial Republicans, said privately that McCarthy had given a "perfectly reckless performance." But the Republicans made no move to rein him in. Joe McCarthy had found his issue, and he would never let go of it now.

The Democrats planned a counterattack. They pushed for a Senate investigation of McCarthy's charges. The Republicans, most of whom assumed that McCarthy was talking nonsense, were still reluctant to abandon the anti-communism issue that had so damaged their rivals. They broadened the investigation and demanded access to a wide range of government employment files, which they believed the Truman administration would not allow. Any confrontation over the files would surely embarrass the President no matter what they contained.

McCarthy was now in a put-up or shut-up situation. He assumed, correctly, that the committee would be stacked with senators who didn't like or trust him. He had to get fresh information to make his charges look credible. Up to this point he had essentially been a loner. Now he went looking for allies, and sometimes the allies came looking for him.

One ally was J. Edgar Hoover, the powerful head of the Federal Bureau of Investigation (FBI). Hoover's power came from his relentless self-promotion, and from the fact that he kept files on practically everybody in Washington. People in government were afraid of him and what he might know about them. Hoover was on his way to becoming untouchable. Though his position was an appointed one, and future presidents hated him, they were afraid to dismiss him. He died in office in 1972, much to the relief of practically everyone. Hoover was a fanatic anti-Communist. He was also a personal friend of McCarthy. They sometimes went to the racetrack together. Some of McCarthy's congressional colleagues, like Richard Nixon, also helped out. So did some journalists. As newspaper publisher William Randolph Hearst, Jr., recalled, "Joe never had any names. He came to us. 'What am I gonna do? You gotta help me.' So we gave him a few good reporters."[3]

Most of McCarthy's help came from a loose network of right-wing zealots who had been warning of Communist infiltration of the government for years. They were people like Alfred Kohlberg, a wealthy leader of the old China Lobby; columnists George Sokolsky and Westbrook Pegler; ex-Communist informers Louis Budenz and Freda Utley; and investigator and conspiracy monger J. B. Matthews. In Joe McCarthy all of these figures found if not a leader then at least a popular symbol. They flocked to him. They opened their files, promoted him in their columns, and in general built him up from an obscure junior senator trying to salvage a damaged political career to a heroic figure in a crusade against the vast and powerful Communist conspiracy, which they were sure was about to engulf America.[4]

McCarthy was also beginning to generate grassroots support. Letters and telegrams were pouring into his office from across the nation. Contributions—large ones from millionaires, small ones from ordinary folk—began arriving to help finance the senator's "crusade against communism." All sorts of people, from disgruntled government employees to out-and-out crackpots, were sending him tips about suspected Communists. And most significantly, virtually every charge McCarthy made, no matter how unsupported or outrageous, hit the front pages of newspapers across the nation. McCarthy was not only accessible to the press, he had also learned how to work the press. He knew what the reporters' deadlines were and how to get his statements out before his opponents had the opportunity to rebut them.

The sudden popularity of Joe McCarthy was not lost on his Republican colleagues. Senator Taft, who disliked McCarthy's tactics and in February had dismissed his charges as "nonsense," changed his tune by April. He ended one conversation with the words, "Keep it up, Joe." And that is just what Joe did.[5]

The problem for McCarthy was that when his charges against individuals were examined closely, they turned out to be anything but sensational. Most of the information was old or vague. The "card-carrying Communists" were nothing more than New Deal liberals. Some had been supportive of the Soviet Union during World War II, but during World War II the Soviet Union and the United States had been on the same side.

Worst of all, from McCarthy's point of view, there were no big names. Some of the people he accused didn't work for the government anymore. Some had never worked for the government. None of them had ever been in a position to influence U.S. policy even if they had wanted to.

Then McCarthy began hinting to the press that he was about to unmask Russia's "top agent." The head of the committee investigating McCarthy's charges, Senator Millard Tydings (Democrat from Maryland), was astonished. He called a closed-door hearing of the committee, at which McCarthy revealed the name of this "top agent." It was Owen Lattimore. He said that he was willing to "stake my whole case on this man."[6] McCarthy went so far as to tell a reporter that four Soviet agents had landed in the United States by submarine and had gone to Lattimore's home for instructions.

Owen Lattimore was a reasonably big fish. He was a scholarly expert on Asian affairs and well known in both academic and government circles. He had never, strictly speaking, worked for the State Department, though he had often advised on Far Eastern policy. He was certainly more important than the clerks and other minor government officials whose names McCarthy had been blackening up to that point.

However, the notion that Lattimore was a spy, or even a Communist, was absurd, and no one knows why McCarthy chose to single him out. Lattimore had been a major villain in the eyes of the China Lobby because he believed that Chiang Kai-shek's Nationalist regime could never be restored to China. Lattimore had advocated working with the Chinese Communists and trying to wean them away from the Russian Communists. Ironically, that was the very policy used successfully by another outspoken anti-Communist politician of the time, Richard Nixon, in 1972 after he became president. But in 1950 advocating such a policy made one a traitor in the eyes of the China Lobby and apparently also in the eyes of Senator Joe McCarthy.

Owen Lattimore is shown during a press conference
at which he is defending himself against Senator
McCarthy's accusation that he was "the top Soviet
agent in the State Department." The Far Eastern
expert declared that if anyone had sworn statements
that he was a red or a red sympathizer, then that
person was "a perjurer and should be prosecuted."

Lattimore appeared before the committee and defended himself ably. McCarthy countered with ex-Communist Louis Budenz, who the senator promised would "expose" Lattimore. But as a witness Budenz could produce no evidence that Lattimore was a spy, and seemed to know little about him. Budenz had been writing and testifying about his past Communist associations for years, but he had never once mentioned Lattimore. He said rather lamely that he planned to in his next book. Budenz was forced to conclude that Lattimore probably wasn't actually a spy at all, and the only real "evidence" that he had was that he disagreed with Lattimore's opinions.[7]

McCarthy had vowed that his reputation would stand or fall on his case against Owen Lattimore. But his chief witness was a bust. No one else who testified was able to produce any evidence that Lattimore was a spy. Nor has anyone found any evidence that Lattimore was either a spy or a Communist in the years since 1950. McCarthy should have fallen—but he didn't.

Instead of providing proof for his charges, he kept making more charges. He then said that he was providing "leads" for the committee to follow up. If they couldn't find the proof, it was their fault. He accused Tydings of being an administration lackey who was conducting "Operation Whitewash." He vowed that nothing would deter him from exposing the "egg-sucking phony liberals" and the "Communists and queers" in the State Department.[8]

The Truman administration finally relented and allowed members of the committee to inspect the State Department's personnel records, something they had vowed not to do. When it was found that these records contained nothing that would support McCarthy's charges, the senator blithely insisted that the records had been "thoroughly raped" before they were inspected and that all damaging information had been removed.

Democrats had expected at first that the hearings of the Tydings committee would last only a few days, during which McCarthy's baseless accusations would be thoroughly exposed as the frauds that they were. Nothing of the sort happened. As the hearings dragged on, McCarthy's popularity continued to grow. A lot of people in America seemed to feel that the Cold War was going badly. China had been "lost." Someone had to be blamed for all of this. Perhaps McCarthy's charges were exaggerated, people thought. But there must be *some* truth in them. And he was doing a good job in alerting the country to the dangers of communism.

One of the many magazine covers devoted to McCarthy during his rise to fame. The bullying tactics highlighted in the newspaper headlines seem to form a halo around the head of the competent looking Senator, perhaps echoing the ambiguity felt by the American public about this man who was bent on ridding the nation of the Red Menace.

5

FROM McCARTHY TO McCARTHYISM

Joe McCarthy's rise to fame and power had been re-markable. From a little-known senator with poor reelection prospects at the start of 1950, he had become, in just a few months, one of the most familiar faces in America. His likeness had been on the covers of *Time, Life,* and *Newsweek* as well as on the front page of every newspaper in the country.

A new word had been coined—"McCarthyism." It meant smearing a political enemy with wild and irresponsible charges. *Washington Post* political cartoonist Herbert Block (or Herblock, as he signed his drawings), a vigorous critic of McCarthy, always claimed that he invented the word.[1] McCarthy himself said that it was the invention of the American Communist party newspaper *The Daily Worker.* In the eyes of the senator's growing legion of supporters, the word wasn't an insult at all. It meant the two-fisted protection of American liberties from "commie spies" and their "pinko" fellow travelers.

Several things had happened early in 1950 to boost McCarthy's stock. On February 3, just before he gave the Wheeling speech, the announcement came that Dr. Klaus Fuchs, a British physicist who had worked in the United States on the development of the atomic bomb, had been arrested in Britain as a Soviet spy. In July, Julius Rosenberg, an American engineer, was arrested in the United States for having passed atomic secrets to the Soviets during the war.

By far the biggest event of the year came on June 25 when the troops of Communist North Korea invaded South Korea. At that time most Americans didn't even know where Korea was. Even military planners had not considered Korea to be of strategic importance. But President Harry Truman felt that he could not let this Communist aggression go unchallenged. In the United Nations the United States asked for and got a resolution ordering troops to Korea. It was supposed to be a multinational UN undertaking, but it was really a U.S. operation, and everyone knew it.

At first the nation rallied around the President, as it always does in time of war, and Truman's sagging popularity surged. That should have been bad news for McCarthy, who had been accusing Truman of being soft on communism. The senator wrote to a supporter: "The war situation makes it difficult to continue the anti-Communist fight effectively—at least temporarily." But he saw trouble ahead for the White House. "I am inclined to think that as the casualty lists mount and the attention of the people is focused on what actually has happened in the Far East, they can't help but realize there was something rotten in the State Department."

His letter concluded, "I still think this is going to be a major issue this fall. . . ." He was talking about the midterm elections.

McCarthy's analysis was correct. The arrival of American troops did not result in a quick and easy victory. By November, when it appeared that the United States had victory within its grasp, masses of Chinese troops poured across the border separating China from North Korea and drove the Americans and their allies back. Ultimately, and after great loss of life, the Korean War settled into a bloody stalemate.

American boys were being killed by the soldiers of a Communist country. Moreover, that country was China, which according to McCarthy had been "lost" to the Communists by traitors in the State Department and other parts of the federal government.

At the time of the North Korean invasion the Tydings Committee was preparing its report on McCarthy. The committee was split along party lines. The Democrats dominated, and the report was harshly critical of the junior senator from Wisconsin. It concluded that McCarthy had perpetrated a "fraud and a hoax . . . on the Senate."

The Democrats had hoped to have the support of some Republican moderates who detested McCarthy personally and politically. But the anti-Communist tide was running too strong. There was an angry, sometimes nearly violent, debate on the Senate floor over adopting the report. In the end the Tydings report was accepted, but on a straight party vote. And despite the scathing criticism, the report didn't stop McCarthy; it didn't even slow him down.[2]

As the 1950 elections approached, Democrats were discouraged and Republicans expected a big win. Joe

McCarthy was not up for reelection. His term had two more years to run. But his new fame had made him a popular and sought-after speaker for other Republican candidates and at the party's fund-raising events.

The Republicans did make gains in the election, and the anti-Communist issue was significant in some races. Richard Nixon, who had been a congressman, won the election for senator from California. He had waged a ferociously anti-Communist campaign against Democrat Helen Gahagan Douglas, whom he dubbed "the Pink Lady." Douglas responded by saying that McCarthyism had come to California.[3]

In the end, however, the Republican gains were not as great as expected. The Democrats still controlled both houses of Congress. But the election was a major public-relations triumph for McCarthy. Several Democratic senators who had been outspoken critics of McCarthy, including Millard Tydings, lost their seats. McCarthy was given credit for their defeat, perhaps more credit than he deserved, for purely local issues played a large part in all the races. The election still added to the widespread belief that crossing Joe McCarthy was a dangerous thing to do.

McCarthy kept up his attacks on the Democrats, whom he now often called "Comiecrats." A particular target was Secretary of State Dean Acheson. Educated at elite schools, Acheson was a polished diplomat and looked it. This contrasted sharply with Joe McCarthy, the tough-talking, working-class brawler and ex-Marine, who always looked rumpled and in need of a shave. It was a clash not only of politics but of culture—and McCarthy won hands down. One point at which he repeatedly hammered away was that Acheson had once been a friend and defender of Alger Hiss. For the right wing, Hiss was the most powerful symbol of what they considered to be the treason of the Democrats, the left, and the Eastern liberal establishment.[4]

By 1951 the war in Korea had bogged down badly. General Douglas MacArthur, commander of the U.S. forces in Korea, was publicly calling for more troops and a policy that would push the war to the borders of China and total victory. The Truman administration was concerned that such a policy could result in a wider war that ultimately might involve the Russians and lead to World War III, a nuclear war. The MacArthur policy, Truman felt, was simply too risky. One of the principles of American government is civilian control of the military. The president is commander in chief. He sets the policy, and it is the duty of the military to carry it out and not to criticize the policy if they don't like it. Truman was furious at what he regarded as MacArthur's failure to obey his orders, and relieved him of his command in Korea.

MacArthur, who had commanded U.S. troops in the Pacific during World War II, was a folk hero to the American people. His dismissal set off a near hysterical reaction. It was denounced by all Republicans and many Democrats. Characteristically, Joe McCarthy went further than anyone else. He implied that the President not only had been under Communist influence but also had been drunk when he fired MacArthur.[5] McCarthy may have regretted that remark, but as usual he refused to apologize.

After he fired MacArthur, Harry Truman saw his popularity sink to its lowest point. MacArthur returned to America almost as a conqueror. His progress from

General Douglas MacArthur, who had commanded US troops in the Pacific during World War II, was a folk hero to the American people. He is shown here at a 1951 Chicago MacArthur Day parade, attended by an estimated 4,500,000 people, the biggest turnout in the city's history.

California, where he landed on his return to America, across the country to Washington, where he made an emotional farewell speech to Congress, was virtually a triumphal march. But history has reversed the judgments of that moment. Today it is the once-despised Truman who has the status of a folk hero. General MacArthur is considered by many political and military observers to have been a vain, arrogant, and rigid man.

One peculiarity of McCarthy's conduct was that while he might appear almost violently angry in public, in private he didn't want to be disliked. He might yell at a man during a debate, and accuse him of betraying the country. But once the reporters went away he might go over to that man, shake his hand, slap him on the back, and wink at him, as if to say, "It's all politics, don't take it seriously." One incident with Dean Acheson became famous. After MacArthur's dismissal, McCarthy stepped up his attacks on the secretary of state. Ironically, the two had never actually met. Then just a few days after the senator had delivered a diatribe in which he described Acheson as a criminal who had needlessly sent American boys to their deaths, and told him to go to Russia, they came face to face for the first time in a Senate elevator. McCarthy stuck out his hand and said, "Hello, Mr. Secretary." The next day the *Washington Post* had a picture of the two standing together. McCarthy had a big smile on his face. Acheson, who was known to never lose his composure, "appeared to be sucking an invisible lemon," according to one observer.[6]

But McCarthy wasn't always friendly in face-to-face encounters. Sometimes he could try to physically intimidate his enemies. At a public meeting he pointed out a reporter who had written hostile stories, and the pro-McCarthy crowd almost attacked the poor fellow.

A more serious incident took place on December 13, 1950. There was a birthday party for Washington columnist Drew Pearson at Washington's plush Sulgrave Club. The hostess, who enjoyed creating excitement, had also invited McCarthy. When McCarthy first came to Washington, he and Pearson had been good friends. But after the Wheeling speech their relationship had soured, and by the end of 1950 they hated one another and made no secret of it. McCarthy had been drinking, and at one point insulted and then attacked Pearson, who was both older and smaller than the senator, knocking him to the ground. Richard Nixon broke up the fight, but Pearson was forced to leave his own party. "If I hadn't pulled McCarthy away, he might have killed Pearson," Nixon later said.[7]

The next morning the Washington press printed a blow-by-blow account of the incident. Opinions are divided over whether McCarthy just got into a drunken brawl, or whether the attack on the columnist was a planned publicity stunt. Pearson had made a lot of enemies around Washington. After the fight about twenty senators called McCarthy to congratulate him. Throughout the nation McCarthy's fans loved his rough-house tactics.

In mid-June 1951, Joe McCarthy made his boldest accusation yet. He announced that he had uncovered "a conspiracy so immense and an infamy so black as to dwarf any previous venture in the history of man." Truman and Acheson were part of the conspiracy, but at its center, the senator said, was General George Catlett Marshall.

This was a shocking charge. It was one thing to attack a politician, or an academic, but quite another to attack one of the generals who had led the United States to victory in World War II. General Marshall was widely known and respected. He had been army chief of staff during World War II and had coordinated the Normandy invasion on D Day. He had served as President Truman's secretary of state and later as secretary of defense. He proposed the European Recovery Plan, which came to be known as the Marshall Plan, generally considered one of the most successful efforts of U.S. foreign policy.[8]

Marshall had his enemies, as every public figure has. Chief among them was General Douglas MacArthur, the Republicans' favorite general. It was widely rumored that Marshall had been instrumental in MacArthur's dismissal. The two generals had certainly clashed in the past. Among some MacArthur supporters the feeling was, "All right, you've gotten our general; now we're going to get yours."

When the Democrats heard that McCarthy was going to deliver an attack on Marshall in the Senate on June 14, they boycotted the session. In the speech, which was nearly 60,000 words long, McCarthy came very close to accusing General Marshall of being a traitor. "If Marshall were merely stupid," he said, "the laws of probability would dictate that part of his decisions would serve America's interests. . . . I do not think that this monstrous perversion of sound and understandable national policy was accidental."

While McCarthy's hard core of regular supporters in the press praised his attack on Marshall, press criticism in general was severe. The senator's speech was

To attack a figure as widely known and respected
as General George C. Marshall was considered
risky and foolhardy even by some of McCarthy's

called "vicious and inexcusable" and "a stink bomb." Republican moderates, who had backed away from criticizing McCarthy in the past because of the senator's popularity and for reasons of party loyalty, now spoke out. Senator Leverett Saltonstall (a Republican from Massachusetts) called the speech, "sickening, simply disgusting." Even conservative Republicans did not leap to McCarthy's defense.

Republican leader Senator Robert Taft was on the spot. He had privately dismissed McCarthy's charges as "bunk," but he hesitated to offend McCarthy's more fanatic supporters. Taft wanted the Republican nomination for president. He didn't want to offend anyone in the party who might help him attain the prize. So Taft waited until October before issuing a mild criticism of the senator. "There are certain points on which I wouldn't agree with McCarthy," he told a reporter.[9]

But even this provoked a flood of angry letters from McCarthy supporters. Taft backed off his criticism, issuing a form letter on the subject of McCarthy that was so vague and contradictory, it was impossible to tell where he stood. That, of course, was the whole idea.

It was clear that in the 1952 presidential election Joe McCarthy and McCarthyism was going to be an issue. It was less clear whether he would be an issue that would help or hurt the Republicans.

6

"ALGER—I MEAN ADLA

As the 1952 presidential election approached, Harry Truman determined that he wouldn't be able to pull off the sort of electoral upset that he had in 1948. Battered by the unpopular Korean War, scandals, and McCarthyism, there was a possibility that he would even be denied his party's nomination. So at the end of March he announced that he would not seek reelection.

Relieved Democrats chose as their standard-bearer Adlai Stevenson, the popular governor of Illinois. Stevenson was intelligent, witty, and highly regarded. But he didn't stand a chance, for the Republican candidate was another World War II hero, General Dwight David Eisenhower, affectionately known as "Ike."

The GOP nomination by rights should have gone to Senator Robert Taft. He had long been considered an effective legislator and congressional leader for the Republicans, even by those who opposed him. Politically he represented the dominant conservative wing of the Republican party. And he sorely wanted the nomination. Eisenhower, on the other hand, was barely a Republican at all. Before the Republicans nominated him, his political preference was unknown. He had been courted by both the Democratic and Republican parties and could have run comfortably in either party. Eisenhower liked to consider himself "above politics." It was the Republican moderates who convinced him to seek the Republican nomination.

The conservative core of the Republican party was with Taft, but they had been out of power for twenty years and desperately wanted a presidential win. So they went with Eisenhower—as near a sure thing as one can get in politics. But to appease the unhappy conservatives in the party, the Republicans chose as Eisenhower's running mate a conservative young senator from California who had made his reputation fighting domestic communism—Richard M. Nixon.

Joe McCarthy won by a landslide victory in the Wisconsin primary election, and felt quite confident that his victory in the general election was assured. The national Republican party agonized over how to handle him during the election. McCarthy had both supporters and enemies. The big problem for the Republicans was that one of his enemies was Dwight Eisenhower. Ike had detested McCarthy ever since his denunciation of George C. Marshall, his former chief of staff. Eisenhower did not make any public statements about McCarthy, but his feelings were well known to Republican insiders, and to McCarthy himself.

As leader of the party, Eisenhower was committed to support all the Republican candidates who were up for election. Still, during the campaign he defended General Marshall in some of his speeches. However, on a campaign swing through Wisconsin he dropped his references to Marshall from his speech. He was persuaded that this would needlessly anger McCarthy supporters. It was a decision that Eisenhower said later he regretted very much. Truman was enraged; he had called Marshall "the greatest living American." The decision not to defend Marshall in McCarthy's home state ended any chance that Eisenhower would be able to establish a cordial relationship with the outgoing president. That was something Eisenhower very much had wanted to do.[1]

If Eisenhower wasn't going to criticize McCarthy in public, he didn't want to embrace him either. He had already had an embarrassing experience in Indiana. There he was campaigning with William Jenner, the Republican senator from Indiana. Senator Jenner was a close ally of McCarthy, and he had also denounced General Marshall as "a front man for traitors." Eisenhower shared the platform with Jenner, but he was cool and distant. After one meeting, however, Jenner rushed forward and caught Eisenhower in a bear hug. Eisenhower was embarrassed. Later he told an aide, "I felt dirty from the touch of the man."[2]

In Wisconsin, Eisenhower made sure that McCarthy did not ambush him with a hug as Jenner had done. He arranged things so that an aide always stood between him and the senator. When they were forced to shake hands, Eisenhower stood as far away from McCarthy as possible. The general public probably was not aware of this subtle body language. But those who followed the campaign closely knew what was going on.

After his big primary win McCarthy felt secure enough to take time out to campaign for other Republicans who asked for his help. His own campaign fund had so much money that he was able to make contributions to the campaigns of other Republicans who were his allies.

McCarthy also felt well enough to go out and campaign vigorously. It had been a difficult year physically for him. In June he had been in the hospital for a sinus operation. In July he was hospitalized again, this time for a hernia operation. More significantly he began to show signs of alcoholism. He started drinking early in the morning and was believed to always carry a bottle with him. He developed a slight tremor of the hands and head. The drinking also gave him almost constant indigestion. He gulped huge handfuls of antacid. One reporter saw him swallow half a stick of butter at a party.

"Oh, this helps me hold my liquor better," McCarthy explained.[3]

But by September he was on the road campaigning for his "friends," like Barry Goldwater, who was running for his first term as senator from Arizona. He even campaigned for candidates who were not his friends. One was Prescott Bush, father of George Bush, who was later to become president. Prescott Bush was running for the Senate from Connecticut. He was a very proper, Eastern establishment, moderate Republican. Not McCarthy's sort of man at all. But he was running against Senator William Benton, one of McCarthy's sharpest critics in the Senate, who had created problems for Joe by raising questions about some questionable financial dealings in the past.

Bush was appalled by the sort of crowd that McCarthy attracted. He described them as "a wild bunch of monkeys." He said his knees were shaking when he had to address them. But he found the personal McCarthy very different from the public McCarthy. And much to his surprise he found himself liking Joe.[4]

But McCarthy did not campaign in Massachusetts. Here another pillar of the Eastern Republican establishment, Henry Cabot Lodge, was trying to fend off a strong challenge from a well-financed young contender named John Fitzgerald Kennedy. McCarthy and Kennedy had already met briefly during the war. John Kennedy certainly didn't agree with McCarthy, and he didn't like him personally. But his millionaire father, Joseph P. Kennedy, liked McCarthy a lot. The elder Kennedy was a Democrat, but a very conservative one. He had contributed to McCarthy in the past. There were rumors that Joe Kennedy persuaded Joe McCarthy to stay out of the Massachusetts race so as not to hurt his son. The truth of the rumors is impossible to determine. It may be significant that John Kennedy never denounced McCarthy or McCarthyism during the campaign, as so many other Democrats did. But the main reason McCarthy stayed out of Massachusetts was Lodge himself. He thought that Joe would hurt him among moderates, and would not be much help for him among Catholics, who were already solid for Kennedy anyway.[5]

Joe McCarthy's most memorable moment in the 1952 campaign came on October 27. He gave a televised speech from Chicago. He slandered Adlai Stevenson with all of the now familiar McCarthy tricks, including the claim that he had documentation proving

Senator McCarthy waves a document in the air as he delivers a "report" on Democratic Presidential candidate Adlai Stevenson. Addressing a dinner audience of 1,400, McCarthy charged that Stevenson endorsed "the suicidal Kremlin-shaped policies of this nation."

Stevenson's devotion to Communists and Communist causes. As usual he had no documentation. He also uttered a well-planned slip of the tongue that became famous. He said "Alger—I mean Adlai"—which was followed by a nervous giggle. The audience loved it, and McCarthy liked it so well that he used the "slip" a second time.[6]

The Eisenhower camp reportedly was embarrassed by the McCarthy speech, and were grateful that the whole thing had not been televised. By this point in the campaign, Stevenson was so battered and exhausted that he didn't even respond to the McCarthy attack.

The election resulted in a landslide for Eisenhower. The Republicans also captured both houses of Congress. They were in complete control in Washington, for the first time since before the election of Franklin D. Roosevelt. McCarthy won reelection in Wisconsin, but his margin of victory was far less than had been expected. He ran well behind the rest of the Republican ticket. It is possible that had it not been for the Eisenhower landslide, Joe McCarthy never would have been returned to the Senate for a second term.

McCarthy's campaign efforts in other states did not seem effective either. Some of his closest supporters, for whom he had campaigned hard, were defeated. Others, like Goldwater and Jenner, were carried into office on Eisenhower's coattails. It could be argued that a strong McCarthy backing actually hurt more than helped candidates, though McCarthy and his supporters certainly didn't interpret the election results that way.

McCarthy's decision to stay out of the Massachusetts race probably did help John Kennedy, who won a narrow victory over Lodge. He was one of the few new Democrats to withstand the Eisenhower landslide.

Some of McCarthy's fiercest senatorial critics, like William Benton, had been defeated. *Newsweek* magazine spoke of the "political scalps dangling from his [McCarthy's] belt." Despite the figures from the election, the general impression in Washington and indeed around the country was that Joe McCarthy was still a dangerous man to have as an enemy. Even if McCarthy's support wasn't as broad as had been imagined, he still had a substantial core of supporters in the United States who were fiercely dedicated to his anti-Communist crusade. For them Joe McCarthy could do no wrong.[7]

But now the field of battle had changed. Up until the 1952 elections McCarthy could rail against the Communist influence in the federal government because the federal government was controlled by the Democrats. Now the Republicans were in control. If he were to attack the federal government he would be, in effect, attacking his own party. The question was whether McCarthy could move from opposition to leadership. That question concerned the Eisenhower administration and the Republican congressional leadership as they moved to take up the reins of power in 1953.

7

COHN
AND SCHINE

When Eisenhower moved into the White House, some predicted that he would act aggressively to cut McCarthy down to size. At his inauguration Ike had given General George Marshall a place of honor. But Eisenhower had determined that his policy toward McCarthy would be to ignore him. No matter what he did or said, just ignore him. That was not a courageous decision, but it may have been a politically wise one. Although Ike was enormously popular, the Republican control of Congress was razor thin. If the President were to pick a fight with McCarthy, that would alienate some of his supporters in Congress—who didn't trust Eisenhower anyway. And this in turn could cripple the entire administration.

The congressional leadership, on the other hand, did not have the luxury of ignoring McCarthy. They didn't want him running around investigating *their*

White House and *their* State Department. They wanted somehow to neutralize him.

By rights and logic, chairmanship of the powerful Internal Security Subcommittee, the chief Communist-hunting group in the Senate, should have gone to McCarthy. The leaders, however, gave it to Senator William Jenner. Jenner's views were almost identical to McCarthy's. He had also denounced General Marshall, and he was the man whose bear hug made Eisenhower feel "dirty" during the campaign. But the Republican leadership saw Jenner as more of a team player, someone who was easier to control. He was also dull, not the sort to attract attention as McCarthy inevitably did.

McCarthy was given the chairmanship of the relatively unimportant Committee on Government Operations and of its permanent subcommittee on investigations. This committee usually investigated such things as waste and corruption. McCarthy accepted the position with apparent gratitude. Senator Robert Taft, the new majority leader, said, "We've got Joe where he can't do any harm."[1] Taft lived only a few more months, not long enough to find out how wrong he was.

McCarthy knew that his subcommittee on investigations had broad powers to scrutinize "government activities at all levels." That authority had rarely been used in the past, but McCarthy fully realized its potential. He could hold hearings, issue subpoenas, threaten to issue contempt citations, and put out reports. An aggressive chairman could claim the right to investigate practically anything in the government. McCarthy engineered a whopping increase in his subcommittee's budget and filled the Republican seats with senators known to be his loyal supporters.

One of the first things McCarthy did was to hire a new staff for his subcommittee. Joseph Kennedy recommended his son Robert F. "Bobby" Kennedy, twenty-seven, for the job of chief counsel. At this point in his career the ambitious and aggressive young Kennedy could properly be described as a McCarthyite. He retained a fondness for the senator until the end.[2]

There was another candidate for the job, the even younger and more aggressive New York attorney Roy M. Cohn. The son of a New York state judge with good Democratic party connections, he became an assistant U.S. attorney at the age of twenty-one. Cohn quickly involved himself with a number of high-profile internal-security cases, including the Rosenberg spy case. He was well off, well connected, and a tireless self-promoter. At the age of twenty-three he was already something of a celebrity. Many nights he could be found at the Stork Club, a posh New York nightclub, mixing with the rich, famous, and powerful.

Roy Cohn was favored by New York ultraconservatives like the columnist Walter Winchell. At the age of twenty-five he became McCarthy's chief counsel, the youngest in such a post in Washington. Bobby Kennedy was given the position of assistant to the general counsel.[3] Ultimately, Kennedy became counsel for the committee's Democratic members. Bobby Kennedy may have had a fondness for McCarthy, but he developed a strong dislike for Cohn.

No one doubted that Roy Cohn was brilliant. But he was also so brash, reckless, ruthless, and rude that he frightened even some McCarthy supporters, who warned that he could become a political liability. McCarthy, however, was devoted to his young counsel.

A young Bobby Kennedy sharing a serious moment with Senator McCarthy as they confer about alleged communist infiltration of defense plants.

Senator McCarthy flanked by staff members
G. David Schine in the background and
Roy Cohn in the foreground.

"You don't know Roy," he told a friend who had complained about Cohn's behavior. "He's a brilliant fellow. He works his butt off, and he's loyal to me. I don't think I could make it without him."

At Cohn's urging, McCarthy created a new position, chief consultant. This unpaid post was filled by another young man, G. David Schine. Schine had once written a six-page anti-Communist pamphlet, which was filled with so many laughable errors that it was obvious he knew nothing about the subject at all. For example, Schine even got the date of the Russian Revolution wrong. The pamphlet was passed out free of charge at the chain of hotels owned by Schine's father. It appears that Schine's only qualifications for office were that he was good-looking, very rich, and Roy Cohn's best friend.[4]

In April 1953, Cohn and Schine, as staff members of McCarthy's committee, made a whirlwind tour of Europe. The stated purpose was to find Communist influence in U.S. Overseas Libraries. In Vienna they looked for books that could be found in both the U.S. Library and the Soviet House of Culture. Among these were the works of the great American humorist Mark Twain. Most Russian readers enjoyed his writings, though some Americans considered them subversive. But to hint, as Cohn and Schine did, that the presence of Twain's books in both U.S. and Soviet libraries was somehow a sign of Communist infiltration, was silly, even in the overheated anti-Communist atmosphere of the time.

In Paris the pair went on a buying spree, charged everything to the U.S. Embassy, and then skipped out on their hotel bill.

To be fair, Cohn and Schine were not the only U.S. officials who traveled in other countries, throwing their weight around and generally behaving badly. But they were the most flamboyant and extreme, and their connection to McCarthy made them instant news.

Europeans were fascinated and horrified by the spectacle of these two brash young men hustling about, ordering experienced State Department officials around, and generally creating chaos wherever they went. Europeans had heard something of Joe McCarthy. Most regarded him as a dangerously uninformed man who through bluster and blunder might involve everyone in another world war. They probably exaggerated his power and influence in the United States. But here were two of his henchmen, running around and acting like they *were* the U.S. government. Cohn and Schine definitely confirmed the worst fears of some Europeans about Americans.

Reporters followed them everywhere they went, and recorded every detail of their brief trip. Though this junket by a couple of young congressional staff members with bad manners had no political importance, it had psychological significance in Europe. The commander of the North Atlantic Treaty Organization (NATO) was asked if the Cohn-Schine visit had been all *that* bad. He replied, "It was so bad it can't possibly be exaggerated. It was awful."[5]

At at least one point during their trip through Europe, a hotel clerk asked Cohn and Schine if they wanted a double room. The pair laughed, and Cohn said that, no, they wanted separate rooms, because *they* weren't from the State Department. This incident touches on another side of McCarthyism.

Most virulent anti-Communist crusaders, McCarthy included, wanted not only to drive Communists and their sympathizers out of public life, but to drive out all homosexuals—"queers" or "fairies" as they were commonly called—as well. McCarthy and others regularly linked "commies and queers" together in their denunciations. The implication was that even if all homosexuals were not Communists, they were still moral degenerates, and this predisposed them to communism. At the very least, they were security risks because they could be blackmailed.

In the 1950s virtually all America's homosexuals were "in the closet," keeping their sexual orientation secret. No one who was openly homosexual could possibly be elected to any public office anywhere in the United States. The mere suspicion of homosexuality could ruin a career.

Secrecy, however, bred rumors. In Washington there was a great deal of private gossip about who was or might be homosexual. The rumors were hard to prove one way or the other, and they were also impossible to stop.

Not all of those who were rumored to be homosexual were left-wingers or liberals either. There was constant gossip about the private life of one of the country's most prominent Communist hunters and upholders of moral purity—J. Edgar Hoover, head of the FBI. Hoover collected, and often leaked, information about the private lives of those he disliked, including their homosexuality. Hoover, however, was a lifelong bachelor. He had no known women friends, though he did have a close friendship with associate FBI director Clyde Tolson, also a bachelor, who owed his career to Hoover.

Hoover was far too dangerous and powerful to be openly accused of homosexuality. Since his death a number of books have supported this charge, but there is no conclusive evidence one way or the other. There is no doubt, however, about Roy Cohn's sexual orientation. Though outwardly he was one of the fiercest haters of "queers," he was a homosexual. He never admitted this publicly, but the evidence is overwhelming. He was well known in the gay world. Cohn died of AIDS-related complications in 1986. To the end he denied that he had AIDS.[6]

Cohn's homosexuality was to become a serious problem for Joe McCarthy. But those troubles were still in the future. At the moment McCarthy was riding high. No matter how outrageously he and his staff might act, he seemed untouchable.

McCarthy now began a series of televised hearings into the activities of the Voice of America (VOA). VOA was part of the State Department's large International Information Agency (IIA), set up primarily to counter the appeal of communism throughout the world. But the VOA had long been a target of ultraconservatives, who claimed that it was "full of Communists." The real problem was that the VOA did not present the view of America that the ultraconservatives held—and from their perspective any disagreement was treason. Now, however, the VOA was under the control of the new Republican administration. This didn't stop McCarthy. The witnesses at the hearings were the usual ex-Communist informers and a line of puzzled and frightened VOA employees.

Nothing was uncovered, but the spectacle provided publicity for McCarthy. The hearings destroyed morale

Staff members of the Senate Permanent Investigating Subcommittee are shown with McCarthy
(*from left to right,* G. David Schine, Roy Cohn ,
McCarthy, Arkansas Senator John McClellan) as
they begin probing the activities of the Voice of
America (VOA).

at the IIA, and the Republican-appointed director and his assistant resigned in disgust. No one in the Eisenhower administration had lifted a finger to help or protect them.

But by the middle of 1953 what came to be called the McCarthy problem was a major topic of conversation at the White House. The junior senator from Wisconsin not only was disrupting the State Department and other government agencies, but he was also frightening the Europeans. The ambassadors to Great Britain and France sent cables to Washington warning of the senator's negative impact on American prestige.

The McCarthy problem was probably best summed up by author Rebecca West, who was visiting Paris and wrote to a friend: "I have been here a week and a situation that depresses me profoundly is driving me into the Seine with a brick around my neck. *You Cannot Believe the Effect of McCarthy on the French Populace.* They do not see why Eisenhower does not take him by the scruff of the neck and throw him into the Potomac."[7]

That was a question many people in America were asking as well. It is certainly what Eisenhower felt like doing. But he still wanted to avoid an open confrontation with McCarthy and his large and devoted following. So he did nothing publicly.

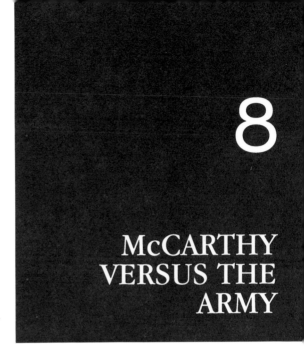

McCARTHY VERSUS THE ARMY

While Joe McCarthy still loomed as an overwhelming and intimidating presence in Washington, hints of serious troubles to come appeared in the summer of 1953.

In June, McCarthy hired J. B. "Doc" Matthews as staff director for his subcommittee. Matthews had been one of the spiritual and intellectual leaders of the far right in America. McCarthy had called himself one of Matthews's "pupils and admirers." Matthews had published *Reds in the White House* and *Reds in Our Colleges.* In July he brought out a companion piece to these earlier works, titled *Reds in Our Churches.* It began: "The largest single group supporting the Communist apparatus in the United States is composed of Protestant clergymen." [1]

Such a statement was neither new nor surprising for Matthews. He had been saying similar things for years, which few people took seriously. But when he became McCarthy's staff director, many people paid attention. The reaction was swift and almost universally negative. Even hard-core McCarthy supporters, particularly those from the South, where the influence of the Protestant clergy was strong, turned against "Doc" Matthews. McCarthy, who almost never backed down, was forced to get rid of Matthews. Even before McCarthy was able to announce Matthews's removal, President Eisenhower issued a statement praising America's clergymen and condemning "generalized and irresponsible attacks" upon them. McCarthy, who usually knew how to play the press perfectly, had been ambushed. It looked as if he had fired Matthews because of pressure from the White House.[2]

Then all the Democrats on his subcommittee walked out and refused to return. Nothing like that had ever happened in the Senate before. It was a profound rebuff.

Joe McCarthy was not about to change his ways. The Republican party and Eisenhower himself tried a variety of tactics to bring McCarthy into line. They used everything from flattery to bribery in an attempt to influence him. Nothing worked. In fact, they made matters worse, for by December, McCarthy was bragging to his friends, "Ike's really leaning. Now he's taking my advice."

But McCarthy had changed in one way. Up to this point, reporters who covered him were never entirely sure that he was serious about his fanatical anti-communism. Often, after making a particularly outrageous speech, he might wink at them. There was a hint of playful wickedness about him. But now he sounded and acted like a true believer. He had convinced many people that an immense conspiracy threatened the nation. Now it seemed as if he had finally convinced himself as well.

The real danger to McCarthy came from an entirely unexpected direction. Something happened in the fall of 1953 that was to have widespread repercussions—G. David Schine was drafted. Despite their flag-waving patriotism, both Cohn and Schine had managed to avoid the draft. McCarthy's persistent enemy, columnist Drew Pearson, kept hammering away at that fact. He pointed out that while thousands of other young Americans were putting their lives on the line fighting communism in Korea, these two young and healthy anti-Communists remained safely out of harm's way. Finally, Schine's draft board reclassified him, and he was drafted and sent to Fort Dix, New Jersey.

Roy Cohn then began a persistent, almost obsessive, campaign to get preferential treatment for his friend. McCarthy was less enthusiastic. He described Schine as "a good boy, but there is nothing indispensable about him . . . it is one of the few things I have seen Roy completely unreasonable about. . . . Roy was next to quitting the committee."[3]

Some of McCarthy's old friends told him that Cohn would have to go. But the senator remained steadfastly loyal. He really did seem to feel that Cohn was indispensable. His attachment to his homosexual aide inevitably triggered rumors that McCarthy himself was a homosexual. In his early days in Washington, McCarthy had picked up the reputation of being a "womanizer." He was seen with a string of different women, contemptuously referred to as "floozies" by his enemies. But there was never any particular woman in his life.

He always portrayed himself as being "a man's man." He never appeared comfortable in the society of woman.

On September 29, 1954, Joe McCarthy married his longtime assistant Jean Kerr, an attractive young woman who was devoted to him. When the marriage was announced, there were whispers that it was an attempt by McCarthy to squelch the rumors of his homosexuality that had begun to surface. Later, when McCarthy and his wife adopted a baby, there were more whispers that this was yet another attempt to hide his homosexuality.[4] Joe McCarthy by all accounts was a devoted parent. But in the poisonous atmosphere of Washington, which McCarthy himself had helped to create, everything was suspect.

In the end, McCarthy supported Cohn's efforts and launched a full-scale investigation of Communist influence in the U.S. Army. This was not McCarthy's first run-in with the Army. Years earlier he had clashed with Army officials over the Malmédy Massacre investigation. This, however, was a more serious matter. McCarthy found a promising-looking case with which to conduct his war against the Army. Irving Peress, a New York dentist, had been drafted and promoted to the rank of major despite his refusal to answer questions on a form relating to membership in subversive organizations. Failure to detect this omission was an administrative error, though most medical personnel in the Army were given the rank of major automatically. Besides, this dentist, no matter what his rank and political persuasion, posed no possible threat to U.S. security. Yet McCarthy professed to see deeply sinister motives. "Who promoted Peress?" became his new battle cry.

Jean Kerr, ten days before her marriage to Senator McCarthy, shown in her Washington home looking over a copy of the pamphlet <u>McCarthyism</u>. The news caption reads, "The pamphlet was written by the Wisconsin senator and Miss Kerr assisted in the proofreading."

Members of the Senate Investigating Subcommittee shown before they met in closed session and agreed to give "high priority" to the case of former Major Irving Peress. *Left to right, seated:* Senators Sam Irvin (NC), Henry Jackson (WA), John McClellan (AR), and McCarthy. Robert Kennedy, whom the subcommittee confirmed as Chief Counsel, is standing.

He also asserted that far from seeking privileges for Schine, the Army had actually offered privileges if the probe were called off.

McCarthy and his staff began berating officers like General Ralph Zwicker. This exchange between McCarthy and General Zwicker at a hearing is typical of what was going on:

MCCARTHY: General, let's try to be truthful. I am going to keep you here as long as you keep hedging and hawing.

ZWICKER: I am not hedging.

MCCARTHY: Or hawing.

ZWICKER: I am not hawing, and I don't like to have anyone impugn my honesty, which you just about did.

MCCARTHY: Either your honesty or your intelligence; I can't help impugning one or the other. . . .[5]

In the end McCarthy ranted that the general was not fit to wear the uniform of the U.S. Army.

Zwicker was so humiliated that he first threatened to resign. Then he told his superior officers that if the Army and the government did not take steps to prevent other officers from being treated as he had been, "the Army will lose materially in the loyal support of its officer corps."

When Eisenhower heard of the incident, he should have exploded. Zwicker was no diplomat or college professor. He was a fellow officer and a friend, one who had served him loyally during the war. Yet the President was still determined to remain aloof. The Army, however, could not remain aloof: Chief of Staff General Matthew B. Ridgeway called Secretary of the Army Robert Stevens and told him bluntly that the Army could not allow its officers to be roughed up like common criminals. Stevens declared that he would do what had to be done. "This is the end of the line," he said.

Vice President Richard Nixon helped to arrange a meeting between Secretary Stevens, McCarthy, and a few other senators. The hope was that Stevens would agree to cooperate with the McCarthy investigation and McCarthy would agree to treat Army witnesses with more respect.

What came to be called the "Chicken Luncheon" was held on Feb. 24, 1954, in the office of the Senate's Republican campaign committee chairman Everett McKinley Dirkson of Illinois. The luncheon included fried chicken, but there was another reason the name was given. McCarthy raged at Stevens, and the secretary simply collapsed. He signed a memorandum of understanding promising to reveal the names of everyone involved in the Peress promotion. There was nothing in the memorandum about treating Army officers with more respect. McCarthy gloated to the press that Stevens could not have surrendered more completely if he had crawled on his hands and knees.[6]

That night Stevens called Nixon in tears. He offered to resign, saying that he had "lost standing." Nixon talked him out of it.

If the "Chicken Luncheon" wasn't the last straw for Eisenhower, it was a pivotal event. The President decided to move actively, if not publicly, against McCarthy. At a press conference he praised Stevens and Zwicker and said that the Republicans in Congress had the primary responsibility for the fair and honorable treatment of Army witnesses. McCarthy shot back immediately. Of Zwicker he said, "If a stupid, arrogant, or witless man in a position of power appears before our committee and is found aiding the Communist party, he will be exposed." He portrayed Eisenhower as being a Johnny-come-lately to the anti-Communist cause.

A few days later Adlai Stevenson went on television and called the Republican party "half Eisenhower, half McCarthy." McCarthy demanded equal time to respond. The Republicans wouldn't let him have it. Instead they chose Richard Nixon to deliver their response. Nixon painted a worshipful picture of Eisenhower, and gently criticized McCarthy, though not by name, for being "reckless."

On March 9, 1954, Edward R. Murrow, the most respected newscaster in America, aired a slashing attack on McCarthy on his popular *See It Now* program. The program consisted largely of film clips of Joe McCarthy in action. It was masterfully done, and the senator came off looking like a brute who terrorized witnesses and patronized the President. Murrow concluded his report:

> This is no time for men who oppose Senator McCarthy's methods to keep silent. . . . We proclaim ourselves, as indeed we are, the defenders of freedom—what's left of it—but we cannot defend freedom abroad by deserting it at home. The actions of the junior Senator from Wisconsin have caused alarm and dismay amongst our allies abroad and given considerable comfort to our enemies. And whose fault is that? Not really his; he

McCarthy's shady tactics eventually became so flagrant that they would have been considered a joke if they weren't so dangerous. The senator frequently provided Herblock with fodder for his *Washington Post* political cartoons.

didn't create this situation of fear. He merely exploited it, and rather successfully. Cassius was right: "The fault, dear Brutus, is not in the stars but in ourselves." Good night—and good luck.[7]

CBS, which aired the program, was flooded with letters and phone calls. Most were favorable, but the responses unfavorable to Murrow were violently angry.

Then on April 22, the Army-McCarthy hearings began. They were the Senate's attempt to sort out the dispute between McCarthy and the Army. Did the senator and his staff try to use improper influence on the Army to obtain preferential treatment for G. David Schine? Did the Army use improper influence in an attempt to derail McCarthy's investigation?

Senator Karl Mundt, who chaired the hearings confidently, predicted that they would be over in a week. He also said that though he was McCarthy's friend and supporter, he couldn't control him. McCarthy kept breaking in with objections of all sorts that slowed the hearings to a crawl. "Point of order, Mr. Chairman, point of order," became his familiar refrain.

From the start it had been the strategy of Army counsel Joseph Welch to keep the hearings going and keep McCarthy on television as long as possible. He believed that the more closely the public was able to observe the senator, the less they would like him. Even before the climactic encounter between McCarthy and Welch over Fred Fisher, the senator's popularity was sagging.

There were many dramatic moments at the hearings. At one point Bobby Kennedy, who was serving as counsel for committee Democrats, nearly got into a fist-fight with Roy Cohn. At another, Ralph Flanders, an elderly and respected Republican senator from Vermont, burst into the hearing room and in front of the television cameras announced that he was going to deliver an anti-McCarthy speech on the floor of the Senate, and he wanted Joe to be there. McCarthy responded by calling Flanders "senile."

The mild-looking Welch was every bit as skillful in the use of the verbal dagger as was the blustering McCarthy. On April 27 a dispute erupted over a photo of Schine with Secretary of the Army Robert Stevens, which had been cropped to make it appear as if the two were alone. It was a small point, but Welch pounded away at it. Questioning a McCarthy staffer, he asked who reproduced the photo—"a pixie, perhaps?"

From the end of the table McCarthy growled, "Will counsel for my benefit define—I think he might be an expert on that—what a pixie is?"

McCarthy was trying to embarrass the Boston lawyer, but Welch turned the tables on him: "Yes. I should say, Mr. Senator, that a pixie is a close relative of a fairy." This was a none too subtle reference to the rumors of homosexuality that swirled around Cohn, Schine, and McCarthy. The room erupted in laughter.[8]

As the hearings dragged on, observers could almost see McCarthy's power draining away. Just a few days before they ended, Senator Stuart Symington of Missouri, a Democratic member of the committee, delivered a furious attack on McCarthy. The audience applauded. Just then the bell rang summoning the members to a vote on the Senate floor. Symington rose to leave. McCarthy shouted, "You can run away if you

Senator McCarthy argues that his cropping a third party out of the picture he had introduced as evidence before a Senate hearing the previous day was "not significant."

like, Stu. You can run away if you like. You shouldn't do that, Mr. Symington. That is just dishonest. . . ." Symington walked out, as did everyone else in the room. No one was listening to Joe McCarthy anymore.

The hearings ended on June 17, 1954, after seventy-two sessions. No conclusions were reached.

Before Welch went back to Boston, he was summoned to the White House. Eisenhower warmly congratulated him on a job well done.[9]

9

CENSURE

The Army-McCarthy hearings reached no conclusions, but there is no question that Joe McCarthy was the big loser. Many loyal members of his staff were forced to resign under pressure. By the summer of 1954, Roy Cohn was gone. Typically he was unrepentant, and left with a snarl. "It has been a bitter lesson to come to Washington and see a reputation, gained at some effort, torn to shreds because I was associated with Senator McCarthy, who has become a symbol of hatred for all who fear the exposure of communism." Those whose reputations had been shredded by Cohn must have been struck by the irony of his complaint.

Cohn went back to New York, where he became a successful and influential lawyer. But he never was truly respectable. He was always getting into some sort of legal trouble. Cohn blamed many of the enemies he had made in the McCarthy days for his troubles. He particularly blamed Bobby Kennedy, who became attorney general after John F. Kennedy was elected president. He said that Bobby was out to get him. Shortly before he died, Cohn was disbarred—banned from the practice of law for violations of legal ethics.[1]

McCarthy did not want Cohn to leave. After his departure, McCarthy's committee seemed to be confused and inefficient. At the next hearing of McCarthy's committee the staff called the wrong witness, because no one had bothered to check his name.

Anti-McCarthy senators were now planning one more blow, meant to be the final nail in Joe's coffin—a vote of censure. There is no official definition of censure in the Senate rules. Though it carries no specific penalties, it is an expression of strong disapproval of a member's conduct. There have been very few votes of censure in Senate history.

After an angry debate and painful political negotiations, the offenses that McCarthy was charged with were limited to abusing the Senate rules. While the charges were narrow, the vote, held on December 2, 1954, was lopsided—67 for and 22 against. The Republicans were split: Conservatives were against the motion; moderates were for it. All the Democrats except two voted for censure. One of those who did not vote was John F. Kennedy.[2] He was recovering from a serious operation and was not in Washington for the debate. He could have made his vote known, but he didn't.

Joe McCarthy's problems were more than political. His health was crumbling as fast as his career. He suffered from all sorts of problems—sinus, stomach, back, and knee. But most of all he suffered from alcohol problems. He was in and out of the hospital frequently. In

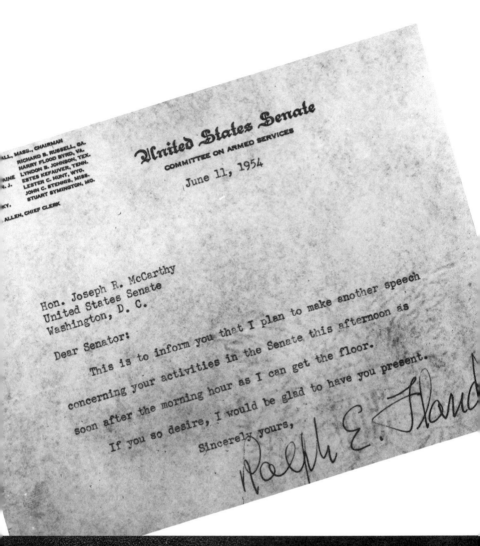

ALL, MASS., CHAIRMAN
RICHARD B. RUSSELL, GA.
HARRY FLOOD BYRD, VA.
AINE   LYNDON B. JOHNSON, TEX.
ESTES KEFAUVER, TENN.
4. J.   LESTER C. HUNT, WYO.
JOHN C. STENNIS, MISS.
STUART SYMINGTON, MO.
KY.
ALLEN, CHIEF CLERK

United States Senate

COMMITTEE ON ARMED SERVICES

June 11, 1954

Hon. Joseph R. McCarthy
United States Senate
Washington, D. C.

Dear Senator:

This is to inform you that I plan to make another speech concerning your activities in the Senate this afternoon as soon after the morning hour as I can get the floor.

If you so desire, I would be glad to have you present.

Sincerely yours,

Ralph E. Flanders

Even as the Army-McCarthy hearings proceeded,
McCarthy was being censured by his colleagues
on the Senate floor. This formal notice was
handed to Senator McCarthy by Republican
Senator Ralph Flanders of Vermont
during the hearings.

fact, he missed a large part of the censure debate. Many announcements and rumors circulated about what was wrong with him. Privately, most in Washington assumed that his basic problem was alcoholism, and he went into the hospital to "dry out" after a bout of excessive drinking.

The censure vote was a serious blow. But McCarthy still had a large and devoted following throughout the country. Even if he was rejected by his own party, he could have started a third party with himself as leader. He might have become the head of a genuine movement in the country. Throughout history, political leaders have suffered far worse defeats and come back strong. But McCarthy didn't even try.

Richard H. Rovere, a reporter who had covered McCarthy and knew him, speculated that the reason McCarthy collapsed was that he really didn't believe in the "sacredness of his own mission." Rovere wrote:

> A man may go a long way in politics—particularly in democratic politics—without much in the way of convictions, but to overcome adversity he needs the strength that can be drawn either from belief in an idea or from a sense of his own righteousness. If he has no convictions, he can scarcely draw courage from them. . . . If McCarthy ever had faith in a holy cause, he lost it early (or acquired it late, too late to do him any good).[3]

The Democrats won the midterm elections of 1954. McCarthy was once again a member of the minority party in Congress. And he was a minority within the minority. He was no longer chairman of the Government Operations Committee, which meant that he no longer controlled the staff, budget, or targets to be investigated. When he rose to speak in the Senate, most of his colleagues drifted out.

For nearly five years a dozen or so correspondents covered McCarthy's every move and recorded his every word. They called themselves the "goon squad." After the censure, the group was disbanded. During McCarthy's glory days his name had been on the front pages of America's newspapers practically every day. After the censure, his name virtually disappeared from the news. Some speculated that there was a press blackout of McCarthy news. Not exactly a conspiracy, but not a coincidence either. Willard Edwards and Sam Shaffer of *Newsweek* said, "Most reporters just refused to file McCarthy stories. And most papers would not have printed them."

After 1955 the White House let it be known that the names of Senator and Mrs. Joseph McCarthy had been stricken from the list of socially acceptable guests. And in 1956 the President invited every senator from either party to a White House dinner dance, except McCarthy. When McCarthy tried to get his candidate appointed postmaster of Appleton, Wisconsin, a minor and completely routine political appointment, the postmaster general, a close Eisenhower associate, turned him down. The administration, which had once feared McCarthy, now delivered the ultimate snub. McCarthy was deeply wounded. Rovere described McCarthy in those days:

> From time to time, he could be seen shambling (or lurching, for he was drinking a lot more and holding it less well) down the corri-

dors of the Senate Office Building, en route to some committee room where photographers and reporters had been sighted. . . . Arrived at a hearing room, he might circle it three or four times—scowling, peering, grinning with effort—to draw the photographers' attention. It wasn't of much use.[4]

McCarthy played no part in the 1956 election. His own term had another two years to run. He didn't even attend the Republican convention, and he brooded a great deal about having been "betrayed" not only by the likes of Eisenhower but also by men like Richard Nixon who were supposed to have been his friends and political allies. McCarthy was also in the hospital again for another of his mysterious illnesses.

Increasingly, McCarthy talked about retiring. He wanted to buy a ranch somewhere where he and Jean and their child could live quietly. He became more interested in making money so that he could retire in luxury or at least comfort. He made some risky investments, which at first seemed to be paying off handsomely. He also made serious attempts to quit or at least cut down on his drinking. But his investments went sour. He lost a lot of money. The Wisconsin friend in whose company he had invested fled to South America. He started drinking heavily again.

Joe McCarthy hit the front pages one more time, on May 2, 1957. He died. The cause of his death was listed officially as acute hepatitis—an inflammation of the liver. The press hinted, correctly, that the real cause of death was cirrhosis of the liver, brought on by heavy drinking.

Holding the flag that was draped over her husband's casket, Mrs. Joseph McCarthy watches as the casket is about to be lowered into the grave at St. Mary's Cemetery in Appleton, Wisconsin.

McCarthy partisans cried that their hero had been murdered, if not directly than indirectly. William Loeb, publisher of *The Manchester Union Leader,* New Hampshire's largest paper, castigated President Eisenhower as "the stinking hypocrite in the White House" who had worn McCarthy down. The *Southern Conservative* said, "Joe McCarthy was slowly tortured to death by the pimps of the Kremlin." Columnist George Sokolsky, who had been close to McCarthy, said, "He was hounded to death by those who could not forget and could not forgive."[5]

His enemies didn't gloat, at least not in public. Seventy senators, most of whom disliked McCarthy, showed up at a service for him on Capitol Hill. Dean Acheson, who had been so fiercely attacked by McCarthy, responded to a reporter's question with the maxim: "Say nothing about the dead except good."

Commentator Eric Sevareid noted, "McCarthy, the political force and symbol as distinct from McCarthy the human being, died three years ago when his fellow Senators formally passed their adverse judgment on his conduct."

On May 7, 1957, services were held at St. Mary's Roman Catholic Church in Appleton, Wisconsin. Joe McCarthy was buried beside his parents in the churchyard overlooking the Fox River.

During his brief fame McCarthy spread a great deal of fear and hurt a lot of innocent people. He made America look frightening and ridiculous in the eyes of much of the world. And for all his ranting about immense conspiracies, he never uncovered even a single Communist.

Joseph McCarthy left behind no political movement and, aside from his tombstone in Appleton, no lasting monument of any kind. But the term "McCarthyism" is still very much a part of our political language. One dictionary defines it as: "the action or practice of publicly accusing individuals or groups of political disloyalty and subversion, usually without sufficient evidence."

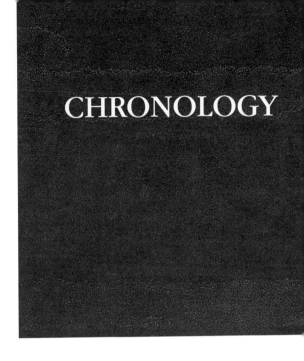

CHRONOLOGY

1908	Joseph Raymond McCarthy is born in Wisconsin (November 14).
1939	Elected circuit court judge.
1941	Pearl Harbor is bombed, and the U.S. enters World War II (December 7).
1942	Enlists in Marine Corps and is sent to the Pacific.
1944	Tries, but fails, to win GOP nomination for senator from Wisconsin.
1946	Wins GOP senatorial nomination and is elected.
1947	President Truman begins loyalty and security program in the federal government (March 21).
1949	Communists triumph in China (January).

President Truman announces that Russia has exploded an "atomic device" (September 23).

First and second trials of Alger Hiss for perjury are held.

1950   Klaus Fuchs is arrested as atomic spy in Britain (February).

McCarthy delivers speech in Wheeling, West Virginia (February 9).

Senate opens investigation of McCarthy's charges of Communists in the State Department (March 8).

Korean War begins (June 25).

Richard Nixon is elected senator from California (November).

1951   Truman fires General Douglas MacArthur (April).

McCarthy denounces General George C. Marshall (June).

1952   Eisenhower/Nixon ticket elected. McCarthy is returned to office (November).

1953   McCarthy hires Roy M. Cohn as chief counsel (February).

Cohn and G. David Schine go on whirlwind European tour (April).

McCarthy fires J. B. "Doc" Matthews (July).

Schine is drafted. Cohn begins campaign to get special treatment for him (Fall).

McCarthy marries longtime aide Jean Kerr (September 29).

1954   Edward R. Murrow airs TV show critical of McCarthy (March 9).

Army-McCarthy hearings begin (April 22).

Robert Welch stuns McCarthy with "no decency" response (June 9).

McCarthy is censured by Senate (December 2).

1957   Joe McCarthy dies (May 2).

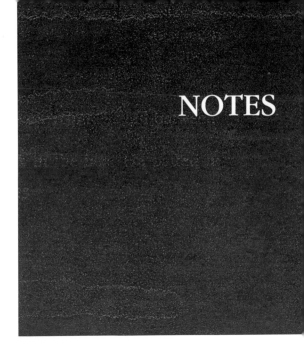

NOTES

INTRODUCTION

1. Richard M. Rovere, *Senator Joe McCarthy* (New York: Harcourt, Brace, 1959), p. 207.
2. Thomas C. Reeves, *The Life and Times of Joe McCarthy* (New York: Stein & Day, 1982), p. 595.
3. Ibid., p. 595.
4. Ibid., p. 629.
5. David M. Oshinsky, *A Conspiracy So Immense: The World of Joe McCarthy* (New York: The Free Press, 1983), p. 464.

CHAPTER ONE

1. Oshinsky, p. 88.
2. Ibid., p. 93.
3. Robert Griffith, *The Politics of Fear: Joseph R. McCarthy and the Senate* (Lexington: University Press of Kentucky, 1970), p. 82.
4. Ibid., p. 85.

5. Reeves, pp. 219–221.
6. Fred J. Cook, *The Nightmare Decade: The Life and Times of Senator Joe McCarthy* (New York: Random House, 1971), p. 97.
7. A scholarly treatment of the complex and controversial Hiss case can be found in Allen Weinstein's *Perjury: The Hiss-Chambers Case.* (New York: Random House, 1978).

CHAPTER TWO

1. There are many different and contradictory accounts of Mc-Carthy's early life. Here I have relied primarily on Oshinsky, pp. 5–6. But the absolute truth can never be known.
2. Ibid., p. 7.
3. Ibid., p. 13.
4. Reeves, p. 13.
5. Oshinsky, pp. 14–15.
6. Reeves, p. 23.
7. Oshinsky, p. 20.
8. Ibid., p. 25.
9. Ibid., p. 33.
10. *Shawango Evening Leader,* July 27, 1944, p. 1.

CHAPTER THREE

1. Oshinsky, p. 44.
2. Reeves, p. 68.
3. Oshinsky, p. 49.
4. Ibid., p. 53.
5. Ibid., pp. 55–56.
6. Ibid., p. 57.
7. Rovere, p. 106.
8. Oshinsky, p. 65.
9. Reeves, pp. 161–165.
10. McCarthy's use of the anti-Communist theme before the January 7 dinner has been described in detail, particularly by Reeves.

CHAPTER FOUR

1. Exactly what McCarthy said at Wheeling is in dispute. See Reeves, pp. 223–230.
2. Rovere, p. 127.
3. Oshinsky, p. 117.
4. Ibid., p. 119.
5. Reeves, p. 269.
6. *The New York Times,* March 24–30, 1950.
7. Oshinsky, p. 149.
8. Ibid., p. 157.

CHAPTER FIVE

1. Oshinksy, p. 158.
2. Reeves, pp. 313–314.
3. Ibid., p. 332.
4. Oshinsky, pp. 190–196.
5. *The Milwaukee Journal,* April 12, 1951, p. 1.
6. *The Washington Post,* June 2, 1951, p. 1.
7. Oshinsky, pp. 179–180.
8. Rovere, pp. 170–173.
9. Oshinsky, p. 201.

CHAPTER SIX

1. Reeves, p. 435.
2. Ibid., p. 437.
3. Oshinsky, p. 232.
4. Ibid., p. 239.
5. Ibid., pp. 239–241.
6. Reeves, p. 243.
7. Ibid., p. 245.

CHAPTER SEVEN

1. Rovere, p. 188.
2. Reeves, p. 462.

3. Ibid., pp. 463–464.
4. Ibid., pp. 255–256.
5. Oshinsky, p. 279.
6. Nicholas Von Hoffman, *Citizen Cohn* (New York: Doubleday, 1988), p. 228.
7. Oshinsky, p. 299.

CHAPTER EIGHT

1. *The American Mercury,* July 1953, pp. 14–26.
2. Oshinsky, p. 320.
3. Reeves, p. 382.
4. Oshinsky, p. 329.
5. Reeves, p. 543.
6. Oshinsky, p. 385.
7. Joseph Wershba, "Murrow vs. McCarthy: See it Now," *The New York Times Magazine,* March 4, 1979, pp. 32–37.
8. Oshinsky, p. 427.
9. Reeves, p. 636.

CHAPTER NINE

1. For information on the remainder of Roy Cohn's career see Von Hoffman.
2. Oshinsky, p. 493–495.
3. Rovere, p. 253–254.
4. Ibid., p. 240.
5. Ibid., p. 251.

BIBLIOGRAPHY

Buckley, William F., and L. Brent Bozell. *McCarthy and His Enemies*. Chicago: Henry Regnery, 1954.

Cohn, Roy M. *McCarthy*. New York: New American Library, 1968.

Cook, Fred J. *The Nightmare Decade: The Life and Times of Senator Joe McCarthy*. New York: Random House, 1971.

Donovan, Robert. *Eisenhower, The Inside Story*. New York: Harper, 1956.

Ferrell, Robert. *Off The Record: The Private Papers of Harry S. Truman*. New York: Harper, 1980.

Feverlicht, Robert S. *Joe McCarthy and McCarthyism: The Hate That Haunts America*. New York: McGraw-Hill, 1972.

Halberstam, David. *The Powers That Be*. New York: Knopf, 1978.

Hirschfeld, Burt. *Freedom in Jeopardy: The Story of the McCarthy Years*. New York: Messner, 1969.

Larson, Arthur. *Eisenhower, The President Nobody Knew.* New York: Scribner's, 1978.

Latham, Earl. *The Meaning of McCarthyism.* New York: Heath, 1965.

Mazo, Earl. *Richard Nixon: A Personal and Political Portrait.* New York: Harper, 1959.

Miller, Merle. *Plain Speaking: An Oral Biography of Harry S. Truman.* New York: Berkley, 1974.

Oshinsky, David M. *A Conspiracy So Immense: The World of Joe McCarthy.* New York: The Free Press, 1983.

Reeves, Thomas C. *The Life and Times of Joe McCarthy.* New York: Stein & Day, 1982.

Rovere, Richard M. *Senator Joe McCarthy.* New York: Harcourt, Brace, 1959.

Sandberg, Peter Lars. *Dwight D. Eisenhower.* Mankato, Minn.: Chelsea House, 1986.

Thomas, Lately. *When Even Angels Wept.* New York: Morrow, 1973.

Von Hoffman, Nicholas. *Citizen Cohn.* New York: Doubleday, 1988.

Watkins, Arthur. *Enough Rope.* Englewood Cliffs, N.J.: Prentice-Hall, 1969.

Wechsler, James. *The Age of Suspicion.* New York: Random House, 1953.

Whalen, Richard. *The Founding Father: The Story of Joseph P. Kennedy.* New York, 1964.

Winchell, Walter. *Winchell Exclusive.* Englewood Cliffs, N.J.: Prentice-Hall, 1975.

Zion, Sidney, ed. *The Autobiography of Roy Cohn.* Secaucus, N.J.: Lyle Stuart, 1988.

INDEX

Protestant churches, 10, 91, 92

Reagan, Ronald, 19
Real estate lobby, 46–47
Republic of China (Nationalists), 21–22, 56
Ridgeway, Matthew B., 98
Roosevelt, Franklin Delano, 16, 17, 30, 31, 41
Rosenberg, Julius, 62
Rovere, Richard H., 108–110
Russian Revolution, 15

Saltonstall, Leverett, 71
Schine, G. David, *84*, 85–86, *89*, 93, 97, 101, 102
Sevareid, Eric, 112
Shaffer, Sam, 109
Soft-drink industry, 46
Sokolsky, George, 54, 112
Soviet Union, 15–17, 22–23, 55, 56, 62
State Department, 10, 51–52, 56, 58–59, 62, 63, 86, 90
Stevens, Robert, 98, 102
Stevenson, Adlai, 72, 76, 78, 99
Sugar issue, 45–46

Symington, Stuart, 102, 104

Taft, Robert, 53, 55, 71–73, 81
Thomas, J. Parnell, 18
Time, 60, 61
Tolson, Clyde, 87
Truman, Harry S., 16–18, 21, 22, 53, 62, 65, 67, 68, 72, 74
Twain, Mark, 85
Tydings, Millard, 56, 58, 64

United Nations, 62
Utley, Freda, 54

Voice of America (VOA), 88

Welch, Joseph N., 10–12, 101, 102, 104
Werner, Edgar, 31–33
West, Rebecca, 90
Wiley, Alexander, 37
Winchell, Walter, 82
World War II, 16–17, 23, 34, 35, 36–38, 47, 55

Zwicker, Ralph, 97–99